The Theory Of Investment And Speculation

Rollin Edson Smith

The Theory

OF

Investment and Speculation

" He that had received the five talents went and traded
with the same, and made them other five talents."

BY

ROLLIN E. SMITH

Member of the Chicago Board of Trade and the
Minneapolis Chamber of Commerce
Formerly associate editor of the Northwestern Miller
and managing editor of the Commercial West

MINNEAPOLIS, MINNESOTA

1904

PRESS OF HAHN & HARMON
MINNEAPOLIS

PREFACE.

"The Theory of Investment and Speculation" is the result of years of close study and analysis of market conditions, made necessary while the author was associate editor of the "Northwestern Miller," and later, managing editor of the "Commercial West."

The writer has had a close acquaintance with many prominent bankers, brokers, millers and elevator owners, as well as with successful speculators; furthermore, he has had some experience in "the pit;" and the conclusion arrived at, as a result of observation and experience, is that speculation is a business, and that it must be learned from the beginning to be successful in it, just as the grain business, milling, merchandising or banking; and that a man must have a faculty for it. A very successful miller might be a poor banker, and a successful broker have no success as a merchant or lawyer. Also, a man may have a thorough and complete knowledge of market conditions and be a good judge of indications and market influences, yet not have the "trading temperament," the nerve, the quick decision, absolute confidence in his own judgment and a liking for the business, which are requisites of the successful trader. All these points are touched upon in a separate chapter.

"The Theory of Investment and Speculation" is not intended as a help to the man of long experience in trading, although he may find in it much of interest and profit. The book is intended rather for the thousands who would not otherwise have the opportunity nor the facilities to gain the information they desire; for the many who have started wrong in their investments, and for the many more who are sure to make simple mistakes, which will cost them money, if they "go it blind." Any man would pay liberally for information that would positively insure his making money. Yet it is a large part of every one's business education to first learn how not to lose money. At the same time, one may be learning how to make it. To those who are willing to take this view of it, this book is intended.

—R. E. S.

January, 1904.

CONTENTS.

THE THEORY OF INVESTMENT AND SPECULATION.

CHAPTER I.

DIFFERENT FORMS OF INVESTMENT.— PRONENESS OF MEN TO SPECULATE.

As long as there is money, and things to eat and drink and wear to be purchased with it, just so long will men use every means possible, varying according to the person, to get it and to increase their possessions. It has always been so, and the possession of wealth has always been regarded as a mark of distinction. This being true, it is therefore natural that there should be a continual searching about for new and sure forms of investment and speculation; and that there should be offered many ways and schemes, legitimate and otherwise, to attract the investor's money. The writer has divided the various forms of investment and speculation into six classes, as follows:

1. Savings bank deposits.
2. Mortgages and bonds.
3. Real estate and farm land investments.
4. Mining stocks.
5. Get-rich-quick schemes.
6. Grain and stocks.

The savings bank deposit is the simplest form of investment, and produces the lowest possible rate of interest; therefore it should be the safest, yet savings banks sometimes fail. The savings bank with its low interest is too often abandoned by investors for "fake" schemes that are largely advertised. As a rule, the patrons of savings banks are not the ones to ever become speculators or to venture much in investments. When they draw their money from the bank, it is likely to be for permanent investment in a home, or because they fear the bank is about to "break," or to "invest" the money in some mining scheme.

MORTGAGES AND BONDS.

Mortgage and bond investments need little comment. There is no better security than a farm land mortgage in the Northwest, provided the loan is conservatively made. Lenders can get 5 per cent net, or more, on their money, and have absolutely good security. There are thoroughly reliable houses that make a specialty of selling farm land mortgages, and who guarantee them. People with a little money for investment, who would otherwise deposit it in a savings bank, might profitably acquaint themselves with reliable handlers of farm mortgages. Bonds may be secured in the same manner. Municipal bonds and those of the well-established railroads are by far the safest.

CITY LOANS.

Loaning on city real estate in growing cities should be avoided, as a general proposition, by those who are not thoroughly familiar with values. The investor should keep his money, and leave this to those who make a business of it. It does not require a financier to give this advice. All that is required is to read the history of such loans for the last 20 years in every city from the Mississippi river to the Pacific cóast; and in earlier days, from the Mississippi to the Atlantic. Growing cities always have inflated values.

During the booms—the late lamented booms—of Kansas City, Wichita, Omaha, Sioux City, St. Paul, Minneapolis, Duluth, Spokane, Seattle, Tacoma and Portland, many hundreds of thousands, yes, millions of dollars were sent from the East to loan on real estate, improved and unimproved, as well as to invest in real estate. In many cases the agents who loaned the money were dishonest, while in others they were honest, perhaps, but "criminally blinded" by the excitement of the boom times. Money was loaned in the most reckless and extravagant manner, the money of people "back East" who had saved and guarded it jealously for years, afraid of any investment more venturesome than a savings bank. Yet they sent it to some agent in a boom town to "invest"!

Building and loan association investments should, as a rule, also be avoided.

REAL ESTATE AND FARM LAND INVESTMENTS.

Although prosperity has nearly overgrown them, the trails of bursted real estate booms may still be followed over a large area of the country, like the trail of a great fire in a forest land years afterward, or the marks of the war throughout the South. In fact, the war hardly left more devastation than the real estate booms of the 80's. The business of cities and communities and states was brought to a standstill, and the man who was not "hard up" was looked upon with wonder, and even suspicion. The whole commercial system of the West had stopped, and it seemed like an impossible task ever to start it again.

All this was brought about by reckless speculation in real estate and farm lands. People argued that the land was there and could not get away. Yet the land got away from them, and their money, too.

A real estate boom is like a prairie fire—the one who starts it may have any amount of fun, but the one who tackles it last gets hurt. Real estate and farm land booms are worked up by agents who want to make commissions, aided by people or railroads with property to sell. They resemble raffles at church fairs—people are first wrought up to the proper pitch of excitement and then relieved of their money. After the bubble had burst in one city with which the writer was familiar, but one man, of all who had touched real estate, had any money or property left.

Real estate and farm land investments made when there is no boom are an entirely different matter from those made during a boom. There can be no better long-time or permanent investment than real estate or farm lands, when made on the right basis. But such investments are hardly possible except for the man who makes a business of it. When he sees investments of that kind, he is not going to give the "snap" away. There are not enough of such bargains nor many such men.

The great objection to land investments, where quick or speculative turns are expected, is that they tie up too much money and there is no opportunity to stop one's loss. A person makes one payment, intending, or expecting, to sell the land before the next payment becomes due. This may be done once or twice, or even oftener; but the next time, the speculator may get caught, find no market for his land—the boom bursted—then he must continue to meet the payments until the land is paid for in full. If he can do this, his money is finally tied up, possibly for years, before the land can be sold even for a small part of the original price.

Like all other forms of speculation, trading in real estate and farm lands is a business of itself, and the inexperienced person who thinks he can "beat the game" during the boom, will, almost to a certainty, lose his money. A real estate boom can no more last, though it may continue for possibly three years, than a bull stock market or a "bulge" in wheat or corn.

MINING STOCKS.

There is not a more legitimate business in the world than mining, nor are there any stocks that pay better than some mining stocks. Yet it is a sad truth that no other business has such a following of fake schemes and palpable swindles. It is safe to say that almost every dollar paid out for stock of mining companies advertised in the papers and magazines is hopelessly lost. There is hardly the possibility of even getting one's original investment back, to say nothing of dividends and a large increase in the value of the stock.

The reason for this is that, in the first place, the stock invariably represents an undeveloped mine, only a hole in the ground. Then, too often, the promoters expect to make their money by selling stock and not by the legitimate business of mining. Again, the promotors are usually men without experience in mining, and such men could not make a success of an already developed mine.

But aside from these factors, the investor is, almost to a certainty, sure to make nothing even if he does not lose all, due to the over capitalization of the company and the large percentage of stock retained by the promoters. Going still further to show the percentage against the investor, there is the honesty of the promoters to be considered, even should the mine prove to be all that is claimed for it. Rather than invest in such mining propositions as are widely advertised, one had much better give his money to the poor; for then he will at least have the happy consciousness of "laying up riches."

Occasionally some friend may offer a chance to invest in a little mining scheme that he and others are promoting. If one has perfect confidence in the promoters, and can lose a little money without feeling it and without regret—how many can?—no great harm can be done, and there is the possibility, slight, of course, of handsome returns.

"GET-RICH-QUICK" SCHEMES.

It seems like dignifying a plain swindle to mention "get-rich-quick" schemes in a work on investment and speculation. Yet the gigantic schemes that have been exploited during the last few years and the success with which the promoters met in getting people's money, seems to justify a brief mention of them. It is not necessary, however, to classify them, for new schemes are continually being brought out. The tenor of them all is, "big profits on a small investment." It may be a building association, a deal in the stock market or in wheat, on the races, etc., or it may be a guarantee of dividends periodically. Yet it is enough to say that no business man is going to give away large profits.

A LEGITIMATE FIELD FOR INVESTMENT AND SPECULATION.

Impatience is the direct cause of the loss of many thousands of dollars every year.

A person has a little money lying idle in the bank, or possibly drawing a low rate of interest. He hears of others making profitable investments, possibly has a friend who has done so, and as he sees numerous brilliant schemes advertised, he finally decides to take a plunge into something himself. Without being thoroughly informed on any class of investment, the most attractive is chosen; which, of course, is the poorest—probably a mining-stock scheme.

How much better it would be to let money lie idle for one, two, yes, ten years, and then to make a highly profitable investment regarding which one has thoroughly informed himself, than to impulsively throw away one's money because the investor "believes it will be a good investment," yet regarding which he has no actual knowledge.

For a certain class of investors, savings banks, farm land mortgages properly selected, and approved bonds are the best. People who do not care to take chances, who are satisfied with a safe investment and small or fair interest, and those who have not the "trading spirit," should be satisfied with such investments.

Yet many people want the opportunity to increase their principal rather than to make it earn interest or dividends, even though they risk losing something in doing so. To those who seek investments that may bring big returns, and to those who desire to speculate, the grain and stock markets offer by far the most favorable opportunities.

The advantages offered the speculator are that these markets are "always there." One can buy or sell, at some price, any business day of the year. In making an investment, one can limit his loss, which is a desirable consideration.

As already mentioned, this cannot be done in real estate investments. As an illustration, the writer will give an experience of a friend. During the boom in a Western city, about 1885, he bought an outlying residence lot, paying $250 down. The price was $1,250. Not being able to sell the lot after a few months, he asked the seller to cancel the mortgage and to keep the first payment. This he refused to do, so the buyer finally paid for the lot in full, paid taxes for years, besides being out of the use of the money. And it is doubtful if the lot would bring more today, although the city has doubled in population, than was paid for it in '85.

How differently a speculative deal can be made in grain or stocks! If one is willing to risk $250, or more or less, he can, when making his investment, deposit the amount as margins, with instructions to the broker to close out his trade should it go against him to that extent. He is liable for no more, and that settles the transaction. To be sure, it may give him a mental "jolt" to lose his money in a day or a week or a month, if the trade goes against him; but how vastly preferable this is to paying four or five times as much, and then having an unsalable piece of real estate on hand.

In this book the writer has studiously avoided saying anything that may be construed as advocating speculation. He has taken the position that people will speculate to a certain extent, anyway; and, this being true, he believes that a book which points out some of the stumbling-blocks will be appreciated by a great number of people.

CHAPTER II.

SPECULATORS AND THEIR WAYS.

Speculators may be divided into four classes, namely, those that make but a few deals, and they very heavy ones, a year; the steady speculators, "the public" or "the country," who are in and out of the market whenever it is active; the "scalpers," either in the pit or around brokers' offices and who make from a few to many trades daily, and the "big professionals," i.e., brokerage or commission houses or members of such companies. These classes hold good whether the grain or the stock market is considered.

Among the big traders mentioned in the first class, there are those who always operate on the long, or buying, side of the market, while others never have any confidence in advances, and therefore prefer to wait until an advance seems to have run its course, then sell short for a big profit. Several well-known Board of Trade men are known to have made fortunes by buying wheat— accumulating large lines of it when it seemed cheap, just as they would real estate, and holding it possibly for several months. Such traders have perhaps two opportunities a year for such transactions, and they may be out of the market for months at a time. This class of trading is really investment buying. Fluctuations of two or three cents are disregarded.

With the exception of the scalpers and the professionals, men who are engaged in other lines of business are the most active speculators. Some of them follow the investment buying plan, operating only a few times a year, while many watch the market daily, and may make several trades a month, or even during a week, on an active market. Those who hold for several cents profit usually make the most money. The writer knew one man who made 20 cents profit per bushel on 10,000 bushels of wheat, not during a corner, either. Such an advance does not come every year, but if it did, very few would get the full advantage of it.

"SCALPERS."

Scalpers, or those who "scalp" the market, taking a small profit or accepting a small loss, are, due to the large amount of trading they do, a distinct advantage to the market. While a considerable amount of such trading is done by outsiders, the greatest volume is of course done by pit traders. As they are members of the exchanges, and therefore do not pay commissions, they can trade on very small margins of profit. Some of them never try for over ⅜c on wheat, and often trade without any profit at all, if the market does not at once move their way. They are also quick to take a small loss when the market goes against them.

When business is dull and orders are few, the scalpers are the salvation of the market; for without them it would sometimes be so narrow that a large order could not be executed without materially affecting the price. Within the last year the writer has seen the wheat pit of the Chicago Board of Trade so dull that an order for a quarter of a million bushels would cause some fluctuation. Without the scalping trade the fluctuations would have been material. With an ordinary volume of business, a million-bushel order would be absorbed without causing a ripple.

"BIG PROFESSIONALS."

What may be termed the "big professionals" constitute a very important factor in all markets. It is they, or some of them, that manipulate the market, run corners and often cause what seems to be legitimate conditions to lose their force. Such men as "Old Hutch," the late P. D. Armour, Partridge, Cudahy, the present house of Armour, Patten and several of the well-known commission houses, might justly be called "big professionals." Such men scalp with millions of bushels, though for wider margins of profit, as easily as the pit traders play with "5's" and "10's." The trade will vividly recall the deal of Armour in May wheat, when, in January, 1903, he "dumped" 10,000,000 bushels or more of long wheat on the market in one day, and continued selling on the following day.

IS THE DAY OF SHORT SELLING PAST?

While it is probably true that the majority of this class of speculators prefers the short, or selling, side of the market to buying in anticipation of an advance, it is true that some of the great

speculators have preferred the bull side. Some
have played each side with success, while others
were at home only on the bear side. On the bull
side, Patten, who makes a specialty of oats, and
the present house of Armour are notable examples.

For many years short selling of grain was a
profitable business, but conditions have changed,
and for the last two years the short sellers have
not met with unrestricted success. Until recently there has always been a "carrying charge" on
wheat—that is, the distant futures were higher
than the near-by months, and all futures higher
than cash wheat. When this was so, a trader
would sell some distant future short, buy it in as
the month approached, and put out his line again
in some still more distant future at a premium.
As long as the futures were at a premium over
cash wheat, the market fluctuations did not affect the trader's profits, for he could always sell
the most distant future at a relative increase of
premium.

Now that this has changed and cash wheat is at
a premium over the futures, the day of the short
seller seems to be over, or at least until conditions
shall have changed again.

In this connection it may not be out of place
to say that this condition—the absence of a carrying charge—was predicted, about a year before
his death, by the late C. A. Pillsbury. He told
the writer, during an interview, that the day of
sure profits for the elevators (a carrying charge)

and the short sellers was contrary to the laws of commerce. No business in the world, he asserted, was entitled to, nor could expect, a sure profit already prepared for it. The miller, the merchant, the manufacturer, and in fact every other line of trade had to work hard for a profit. Therefore it was unnatural that the elevator owner should buy wheat, and, without effort, always be enabled to sell it for some future delivery at an insured profit.

Whether the day of the sure carrying charge and the profit for the short seller will return, cannot, of course, be told. With a very large crop of wheat in this country, it probably would temporarily.

THE GENUINE BULL AND THE REAL BEAR.

The man who is always a bull, who never believes the price is too high nor that, when low, it can remain down, is differently constituted than is the man who takes the reverse view of it—the real bear. Some men always honestly believe that wheat is worth more money—that it actually should bring more—than the usual market price, just as one man can see greater value in a certain horse than other men can. The genuine bull seems always to have in mind the, what he considers, legitimate value of wheat. The bull is a friend of wheat. He seems to take an interest in its welfare, and he cannot understand the views of the bear.

Now the bear, the real, persistent bear, has none of this sentiment. He regards wheat from the position of the auctioneer—it is worth only what it will bring at forced sale. Any price, no matter how low, is never too low for the bear. And whenever it does advance, he is continually predicting its downfall. The real bear honestly believes that 70c, Chicago, is a good price for wheat.

It is these two factors, assisted by the many traders who are continually changing from one side to the other, that cause the wide fluctuations in the market; though added to them is the influence of the cash-grain buying of millers and the hedging of elevators.

CHAPTER III.

LOOKING OVER THE SPECULATIVE
FIELD.

It is a fact beyond dispute that much of the money lost through speculation is lost by men who buy stocks or grain without first giving the markets careful consideration and study.

Some men make money, and others lose it, by trading entirely on other people's advice or suggestions. In fact, some never learn to trust their own judgment; nor do they ever study conditions closely enough so that their judgment is worth anything. On the other hand, it is really surprising how well informed some men, not connected with the trade, become regarding values of stocks and grain.

Everyone who expects to do any trading should at least learn something of values and of the factors that are most likely to affect them. Some men, for instance,—and not a limited number, either,—regard wheat as high at 75c, Chicago, and steadfastly refuse to buy at above that price. Yet certain conditions might make it cheap at 80c, or dear at 70c. It is the same with stocks. Yet in asking the advice or the opinion of some friend regarding wheat or stocks one may get the views of a chronic bear or a cheerful bull, or of one who is prejudiced by speculations of his own. The right kind of a broker

can give many valuable suggestions to his customers, but the man who cannot learn to do his
own trading had better give up attempting to be
a speculator.

The best advice that can be given any one who
is beginning to take an interest in the markets, is,
"Wait." There is no occasion for hurry. The
markets will be here long after the present gener-
ation is gone, and bull campaigns and bear raids
will continue just the same, year after year. A
little study of the markets may save one some
money; it will at least enable him to lose it in-
telligently.

A bull market, whether grain or stocks, at-
tracts a large amount of outside buying. People
buy wildly merely because the market is advancing. Yet it is a self-evident fact that the top is
somewhere, and that legitimate conditions will
finally assert themselves. Now it is these legitimate conditions that the speculator must keep in
mind, and not get too far away from them. Yet
it should be borne in mind that legitimate conditions are not what some one may think they are.

THE STOCK MARKET.

The first thing to consider in looking over the
stock market, is, What has it been doing, in a
general way, for the last year? Then the financial and commercial situation should be studied—
the situation of the whole country,—in the East,
where the manufactories and Wall Street are, in
the Northwest and West and the central states,
where the crops are raised; in the South, where

the cotton is, and then the labor situation as a whole should be considered.

Having satisfied one's self on these points, some study of a few stocks themselves would be advisable, taking some of the most active low-priced ones. At this time, the last of November, 1903, the following are some of the active and well-thought-of stocks—at present the "industrials" are not receiving much attention: "Sugar," "Atchison, com.," " B. & O., com.," "B. R. T.," "Erie, com.," "Mo. Pac.," "Peo. Gas.," "U. P. com.," and "Wab. Pfd."

Looking up the records of these stocks for, say three years, it is learned that in 1901 Sugar sold as low as 103⅛ and up to 153. In 1902, 113 was low point, and 135⅛ high. In 1903, the range was 107⅛ to 134⅜. The present price is around 120.

Atchison com., in 1901, ranged all the way from 91 to 42¼. In 1902, 72¼ to 96⅝. In 1903, from 89⅞ down to 54, with the present price 66.

B. & O. com., in 1901, dropped from 114½ to 81¾. In 1902 the range was from 92⅝ to 118½. In 1903, 104 down to 71⅝, with the present price 76.

All the stocks mentioned should be treated in the same way. A careful person would, before going further, want to know what caused both the low and the high prices in 1901—it happened that the low prices followed the high, a veritable slump. Then, what caused the recovery to high point in 1902 and in 1903, and what was the cause of the long decline of the present year; and are values likely, within the next year, to go back to the high prices of 1902 or 1903.

It should be remembered that the slump of 1903 will have an important bearing, by comparison and as establishing a new basis, on values for several years to come.

After familiarizing one's self with general conditions and the range of prices, the investigator should go into the prices of the stocks selected in detail; and this can be done to the best advantage by means of the chart, explained elsewhere. Some company publishes charts, showing the fluctuations of all the principal stocks, monthly. These furnish a valuable record, and no inexperienced person should think of trading without having this knowledge. Thus equipped, he may decide whether he wishes to venture into the market.

Yet all this is merely preliminary to the actual study of stocks, where one wishes to buy for investment. In fact, it is only a glance at the outside. Should one care to enter into it fully, he can find several books devoted entirely to the analyzing of stocks; and the Wall Street Journal will be of great assistance. One can also get a book giving details, such as mileage operated, capitalization, equipment, receipts, expense, amount of traffic, earnings, comparisons, etc., of all the principal railroads of the country; and similar information regarding the leading industrial and miscellaneous companies.

THE GRAIN MARKETS.

The first factors to consider, in looking over the grain markets, are, the season of the year, the price, recent marked changes, the supplies of this country and of the world, the amount of the last crop and the probable size of the next, and the export demand. Then these factors should be compared with conditions at the same season of previous years. The sentiment in Chicago should also be considered, and whether the market is normal or subject to manipulation.

Wheat, of course, is the principal cereal, though at times corn and oats offer certain advantages and splendid opportunities. It is a peculiar fact that at times there is a marked sympathy between "coarse grains" and wheat, while at other times the different markets will fluctuate independently of one another. Some times wheat "is weak in sympathy with corn;" and again, corn will be "strong in sympathy with oats." At other times, one grain will advance or decline while the others are inactive. There are times, however, when the speculator must take all the markets into consideration. The grain markets decline on fine crop prospects, while the stock market is strengthened by them, for, the greater the crops, the greater the earnings of the roads that haul them. Likewise, a short-crop outlook advances grain prices, but depresses stocks.

The next chapter, "Wheat," goes into the subject of grain speculation in detail; and while it is mostly devoted to wheat, the same principles may be applied to the corn and the oats markets.

CHAPTER IV.

WHEAT.

A STUDY OF VALUES.—THE BEAR SIDE.

Speaking in a general way, the natural tendency of prices seems to be downward. At times it almost seems as though the attraction of gravitation affects prices as it does things of density and substance. As the surface of the earth is the only basis one can be sure of for weighty things, unless there is a solid structure under them, so a ridiculously low price for wheat and other cereals is the only basis one can always feel absolutely confident of. Cash wheat has sold at 50c per bushel in Chicago as recently as 1894, and it sold between 50c and 60c every month of that year. In 1896 it sold under 60c five different months. Yet the crop of the country was only 396,132,000 bushels in 1893, and 460,267,000 the following year. In 1895 and again in 1896 the crops were also very moderate. The low price was directly attributable to conditions that are not, fortunately, often factors in the situation, namely, a panic, general financial distress and fear of a financial upheaval due to a presidential election.

Corn and oats have also made some low records in recent years. In 1897 cash corn in Chicago sold at 21¾c, both in January and February, and in only two months did it sell in the 30's. In the same year, oats sold at 15¾ to 17c in January, and 15⅝ to 16⅝c in February, and sold over 20c only one full month, December.   In 1896 the range was also low, perhaps a little lower average than the following year.   In September, 1896, oats sold as low as 14¾c and at 15c in July.

These figures show what is possible on the low side of prices, due to what might be called natural causes. Lack of speculation may, perhaps, be called a natural cause for price depression; although when speculation is light a few of the "big professionals" and all the scalpers take advantage of the situation to unnaturally hammer down the price.

Without an active speculative market, the price sags below its legitimate level, and so in turn invites large speculative buying.   It is always helped in its downward course by various interests.   The flour buyers, for example, from the small grocer who buys 10 barrels at a time, to the big jobber who buys 10,000 barrels; the flour importer of Europe and the wheat importer, all are steadfast bears and are continually trying to buy a trifle under the market.

It can be said of the American miller, however, whether a small country miller or one of the huge Minneapolis concerns, that he is not a factor in depressing prices. On the contrary: and if all the wheat raised in the country were ground at home, the farmer would receive a much higher average price than when a part of the crop is exported as wheat.

THE BULL SIDE.

On the brighter side, for low prices always seem to indicate gloom, while there is something cheerful about an advancing market—on the brighter side, then, a glance at prices for the last few years shows "dollar wheat" oftener than "half-dollar." Yet it must be confessed that $1 for wheat is almost always the result of manipulation. A small lot of No. 1 northern wheat sold at $1 at Minneapolis during the summer of 1903, as the result of sentiment and a flurry, induced by a shortage of supplies. Yet as only a couple of cars sold at that price, it can hardly be said that a price basis was established.

It is almost inconceivable that wheat futures could sell at $1 in Chicago without manipulation, except in case of war or phenomenal crop disaster.

Some of the recent high prices for cash wheat in Chicago were as follows: In 1890, when in May, $1 was reached, and $1.08¼ in August, and over $1 in September, October and November. In 1891, over $1 was paid in five different months. In 1897-'98, the "Leiter" years, $1 to $1.85 was recorded. Since that time cash wheat has seldom touched 80c, although, in September, 1903, it sold at 95c when the Minneapolis price was $1.

WHAT IS A CONSERVATIVE PRICE BASIS?

The range of prices is of more than passing interest in a work of this kind; for, in the chapters on speculation, it is necessary to refer to it. Speculators and investment buyers must use some price as a unit of value, or price basis, which is raised or lowered accordingly as local and general conditions seem to justify. A study of prices shows that the legitimate price basis, if the term is permissible, is somewhere above 50c, for that price is only possible under extremely abnormal conditions. "Price basis" is understood to mean a price at which wheat can be bought with reasonable certainty that there cannot be a decline of more than say 5c, at the outside, before the price shall again sell at the purchase price. Also, short sellers regard the basis as a price at which wheat may reasonably be expected to sell at again, within the life of the option, no matter how high it may go.

Some men set the basis immovably at 70c, regarding wheat as high at over 75c. This is unreasonable. The basis must be movable, on a sliding scale, to meet conditions from one crop year to another, and from one season to another. At the present time, 80c, Chicago, seems a conservative basis, considering stocks of wheat the world over; the size of recent crops, and the consumption.

Many conservative speculators have another arbitrary basis, above which they will not buy wheat, or only with the greatest caution and under unusual conditions. This, however, will be touched upon in another chapter.

PRICE MAKING FACTORS.

To say that supply and demand make or regulate the price of wheat, is to say what is not altogether true. It is often asserted by farmers' organizations that short selling and speculating in futures continually depresses the price. Yet neither is this true at all times. In fact, there are so many interests in wheat that it cannot be said that any one influence makes the price. In fact, that would be impossible, for there are two kinds of prices to consider—"cash wheat" or the actual wheat, and the futures.

Now the supply and demand does regulate the price of cash wheat to a large extent, but the supply and demand of cash wheat does not make the price of futures, though, naturally, it has some bearing on it. On the other hand, the price of futures has an influence on cash wheat.

The futures are largely influenced by what may happen, but which, if it actually does happen, is soon forgotten and so loses its force. This should always be kept in mind. Damage to crops, threatened rains, or drouth, or frosts, the crop movement, whether large or small; increase or decrease in supplies, war rumors and a hundred other market influences, are discounted as far in advance as the trade can detect them.

For instance, general rains during harvest may advance the price 10c, because "the movement will be delayed." Yet when the rains cease, the trade discovers that the quantity of wheat has not been reduced, and that as the quality has been injured "the poor wheat will be rushed to market;" and this is a bearish factor. Then the traders who confidently bid the price up 10c, as fearlessly pound it down 10c, or possibly 12. It cannot be said that supply and demand has anything to do with this; yet this very thing in a greater or lesser degree, and on one "scare" or another, happens several times a year. Yet as cash wheat follows these advances, the farmer who has any wheat is just as much benefited as if an actual increased demand was causing them.

When the supplies of wheat are unquestionably short of milling requirements—which is a difficult thing to make the trade believe—then the price is for the first time on what is understood as a supply-and-demand basis. Yet this may happen and the futures not be materially affected. This was the case during the summer of 1903. During all of that year, even during the crop movement cash wheat in Minneapolis was higher than the futures. Most of the latter part of the year, one could buy wheat deliverable the following May cheaper than the actual wheat. Yet at the same time it was generally conceded that wheat would be scarce and badly wanted by the mills before May.

During the heavy crop movement, September, October, November and December, the price is expected to rule relatively low. This is taken advantage of by the bears, and the price is often hammered in anticipation of the movement. The price of May wheat is not thought to have established a basis until it has stood the heavy selling of shorts, and of hedging and spreading, which is sure to take place in the fall. During the fall of 1903 the spring wheat movement was light, owing to a short crop—though few would at first believe it was short—yet the "big professionals" were bearish almost to a man, declaring that, although the movement was light, it would increase, therefore the price was too high. It happened, however, that the movement did not increase.

Many of the fluctuations of from one to three cents are caused by the market becoming "congested;" that is, oversold or overbought. When, in anticipation of an advance, the scalpers have all bought wheat, there is finally no one left to buy anything that may be offered. Then a little panic.ensues, if selling orders come in, and "the crowd" begin to "dump" their wheat. This causes a decline instead of the expected advance. The contrary effect results when the traders all get short, so that they cannot absorb any more buying orders.

It is not difficult to account for the fluctuations of the market, yet when this is done one is no nearer than before to a conclusion regarding what really establishes prices. With an average crop the world over, and normal conditions prevailing in all countries, Liverpool is probably the great regulator. And this means that the imports, or the requirements, of the United Kingdom, establish a basis of prices for the rest of the world. Again, this means that wheat-raising countries with an exportable surplus, must, to a large extent, sell their entire crop on a basis of Liverpool prices.

When any one country has a short crop, however, local conditions assert themselves. For example, when Australia had a crop failure in 1903, the Pacific coast sold its crop at nearly double what it would have got had it depended upon Europe for a market for its surplus.

THINGS THAT INFLUENCE THE MARKET.

Under this head, an array so large as to be startling might be mentioned, but the following are the principal factors, besides the speculators themselves, that have an important influence on the market:

The "cables."
Export business.
World's shipments, or "clearances."
"On passage."
Receipts and shipments.
Visible supply.
World's visible.
Crop conditions.
Milling demand.

Of the "cables," or foreign market quotations, Liverpool is the most important, with London, Paris, Antwerp and Berlin following. Liverpool's opening quotations on wheat and corn and those of 1:30 o'clock are received in Chicago and other Western markets by 9 a. m., while the closing quotations come about an hour later. The cables are looked for the first thing every morning by every one interested in the market, yet very often

Chicago will advance or decline without regard to whether the cables respond. However, when Liverpool develops weakness or strength before Chicago, the latter is certain to be influenced, unless it happens to be during the course of a manipulated market. During apparent manipulation, which was frequent in 1902-3, Chicago frequently advanced or declined a couple of cents although the cables came "unchanged" or "⅛c to ¼c higher" or as much lower. Even when Liverpool has been up ⅝c, Chicago has declined sharply. Yet, except in case of an actual corner, or when, by reason of a short crop in this country we are independent of Europe, the Liverpool market cannot be ignored. It is the great regulator.

Next to the cables, every morning, the trade wants to know how many "loads"—8,000 bushels to the "load"—were "worked for export;" for, when the price gets above an export basis, or so much above that the foreigners cannot buy on the little declines that are continually coming, it is argued that it is too high. As a matter of fact, however, the price is seldom actually on an export basis, for as soon as it is known that liberal sales are being made, the scalpers at once bid the price up. This is paradoxical, perhaps, yet the market is full of strange things. The amount of wheat and corn sold, or "worked" for export, so far as can be determined, is reported daily.

WORLD'S SHIPMENTS.

The world's shipments, or "clearances," or the amount exported from all ports, is also an important factor, and the weekly clearances or exports form a part of trade statistics. The world's shipments are given out on Tuesday, as compiled by Bradstreet's, and include shipments of wheat and corn from the following countries: America, Russia, "the Danube," Argentina, India, Australia, Austro-Hungary, "various."

The following table shows six months exports of wheat, and flour computed as wheat, from all ports, for a series of years—the variation from year to year is worthy of note:

Week Ending—	1903	1902	1901	1900
July 2	2,966,682	3,211,215	3,787,639	3,018,832
July 9	2,380,410	4,404,115	5,016,149	2,829,910
July 16	3,652,784	3,775,222	5,221,880	3,029,381
July 23	2,781,988	3,980,969	6,974,526	2,363,743
July 30	3,191,442	4,388,534	6,463,391	3,327,003
August 6	3,040,629	4,244,363	8,831,199	3,318,760
August 13	3,413,191	4,591,805	9,030,701	3,113,641
August 20	3,372,789	5,954,759	6,606,989	2,695,168
August 27	3,245,056	5,436,530	6,607,611	3,248,313
September 3	3,131,839	6,276,299	4,406,064	3,373,100
September 10	3,045,040	5,444,046	6,648,609	4,665,982
September 17	1,909,083	5,435,323	3,840,574	3,535,857
September 24	3,050,430	5,077,070	4,470,352	3,242,810
October 1	4,082,681	6,870,578	6,195,749	4,450,167
October 8	2,378,722	5,645,779	4,719,898	4,292,855
October 15	2,865,610	5,240,688	5,536,073	3,796,643
October 22	4,265,080	7,060,137	4,952,134	4,932,978
October 29	4,094,873	5,997,620	6,672,388	3,612,421
November 5	4,340,281	5,715,555	5,469,645	3,555,507
November 12	3,659,823	4,440,160	4,983,734	4,062,020
November 19	2,974,277	5,277,672	5,518,930	3,827,296
November 26	3,851,767	4,179,685	5,117,478	3,497,880
December 3	4,201,504	5,704,440	4,604,846	3,432,159
December 10	4,590,530	3,761,047	3,879,809	4,785,577
December 17	3,363,035	3,256,037	4,332,832	4,123,350
December 24	2,335,606	3,560,486	4,291,543	3,868,165
December 31	2,915,236	3,336,206	4,818,471	3,914,301

In 1903 the bears argued that the light exports were a bearish factor, while the bulls asserted that they indicated a smaller crop than estimated, which, of course, was a bullish argument.

Another factor of importance, and one to be looked after every morning before the market opens, is the receipts, or "the cars," as they are concisely called on the Chicago Exchange. The receipts at Minneapolis, Duluth, Chicago and Kansas City are of the greatest importance.

When the totals are given in bushels, St. Louis, Milwaukee, Toledo and Cleveland are included. The weekly "primary receipts," i.e., receipts at primary markets, or where the grain comes directly from the country and not from other markets, as at Buffalo, for example, and the shipments, are factors for consideration every Monday, with comparisons with the amounts of a year ago.

Still another factor is the amount of wheat (and corn) "on passage." This is estimated every week. The amount of wheat and corn on passage includes all that is on the ocean, destined for European ports; that which has been cleared from all the export ports of the world and has not yet reached destination. As a record is kept of exports and arrivals at destination, the amount on passage can be closely approximated every week.

THE "VISIBLE."

An item of particular importance is the increase or decrease of the visible supply in America and Canada, as compared with the same date of the year before. The "visible" includes stocks of grain in public elevators only, and not that in private houses. Grain in store at the following points is included in the visible supply, as compiled by the secretary of the Chicago Board of Trade, and given out on Monday: Baltimore, Boston, Buffalo, do. afloat, Chicago, Detroit, Duluth, Ft. William, Ont., Galveston, Indianapolis, Kansas City, Milwaukee, Minneapolis, Montreal, New Orleans, New York, do. afloat, Peoria, Philadelphia, Port Arthur, Ont., St. Louis, do. afloat, Toledo, Toronto, On Canals, On Lakes, On Miss. River.

The world's visible supply of wheat is compiled by Bradstreet's, and is issued every Tuesday.

THE WORLD'S SUPPLY OF WHEAT AND FLOUR.

The visible supply of foodstuffs of the world is estimated monthly. The world's visible supply of foodstuffs includes wheat and flour afloat for Europe, in store in Europe, in store in Argentina, and in store in America. The world's visible for three years follows:

	1903 Bushels	1902 Bushels	1901 Bushels
January	175,580,000	208,430,000	211,100,000
February	163,690,000	210,490,000	208,640,000
March	179,560,000	199,700,000	204,350,000
April	155,560,000	183,320,000	197,000,000
May	135,120,000	158,730,000	180,000,000
June	120,370,000	133,170,000	160,500,000
July	103,530,000	105,820,000	142,400,000
August	93,260,000	95,000,000	138,200,000
September	103,870,000	103,500,000	146,000,000
October	140,930,000	135,500,000	165,000,000
November	159,350,000	174,000,000	177,400,000
December	174,100,000	181,750,000	210,000,000

The cash demand for wheat is carefully watched; also, the milling situation. If the elevator companies and the mills are good buyers, this helps the market for futures. Should prices for cash wheat not follow the futures, then it is regarded as a point against the latter.

GOSSIP.

Gossip about the crops is one of the chief joys of the scalper, those who write market letters, and of the commercial editors. In fact, the receipts, the exports, the supply, and the condition of the next crop are subjects that the trade is never for an hour permitted to forget. This has a tendency to make the trade mechanical in its reasoning. Men get into a rut, and think by comparison—compare every condition with "a year ago." For example, if receipts at Minneapolis or Kansas City run somewhat heavier for a few days than "a year ago," many regard it as a bearish feature, and send out gossip something like this: "Heavy receipts are weakening the market. Unless supported, it will sell lower." Yet the heavier receipts may only be the breaking of a little congestion in the country somewhere, and the average for the week will be normal. It is the same with the exports—unless they are as heavy each week as "a year ago," it is a very bad indication, although this country may not have so much to export as on the last crop. Yet, after all, the speculative public wants "gossip," and it is doubtless this desire that has brought about the system of making much of trivialities.

The gossip that daily comes over the wires should not be regarded too seriously by inexperienced traders.

THE WHEAT MARKETS OF THE WORLD.

Among the wheat markets of the world, Chicago and Liverpool are, without question, the most important; yet Minneapolis is the greatest cash-wheat market. As has already been pointed out, in a previous chapter, Liverpool is greater than Chicago in regulating prices, though the latter "makes" more prices—that is, speculation causes more and wider fluctuations; yet in time the influence of Liverpool is felt, and Chicago is forced into line.

Of the other European markets, London, Paris, Antwerp and Berlin are of importance; but only occasionally do they exert any influence on the speculative markets of this country.

After Chicago, come Minneapolis, St. Louis, Milwaukee, New York, Duluth, Kansas City and Toledo, as the principal grain markets of America. Duluth, Kansas City and Toledo are chiefly cash-wheat markets. Minneapolis is not only the greatest cash-wheat market but at times is next to Chicago as a speculative center.

In theory there should be a difference in price between the various markets, based on the difference in freight rates. Yet there is no relative difference that can be regarded as normal. Chicago is now relatively lower than other markets, because any kind of wheat, excepting Pacific coast, is deliverable there on contract—No. 1 northern, No. 2 red, or No. 2 hard winter. At Minneapolis only No. 1 northern (No. 1 hard is too scarce to mention) is deliverable on contracts, while at

St. Louis the rules of the exchange provide for No. 2 red only. Therefore there might easily be a "squeeze" in Minneapolis or St. Louis that would not affect Chicago; and now that No. 2 hard winter wheat (at 5 cents penalty) is deliverable on contract in Chicago, it is practically impossible to actually corner that market, although this does not prevent manipulation.

The question of the relative position of the various markets properly comes under the head of "spreads," and will be gone into at some length in another chapter.

THE WHEAT CROP OF THE WORLD.

In a good year, Minnesota will raise 80,000,000 bushels of wheat. Of all the wheat-growing countries of the world, there are but nine that exceed this amount. They are, Russia, France, Italy, Spain, Hungary, Germany, Canada, Argentina and India. Roumania raises nearly as much.

A good crop for the Dakotas and Minnesota, which raise most of the spring wheat of this country, is 200,000,000 bushels. Only three countries exceed this amount, namely, Russia, France and India.

The United States is the greatest wheat-growing country in the world by a very large percentage. The largest crop ever raised in this country was in 1901, when 748,000,000 bushels was grown. About 650,000,000 bushels, however, is a large crop, as it has been exceeded but three times.

Russia, including Poland, is second. In 1902 the Russian crop, including Caucasus, was 480,-

000,000. Estimates differ several millions on the total. In 1903 Russia probably raised the greatest crop in its history. The Hungarian minister of agriculture places it at 523,000,000 bushels; yet as this estimate was made in the fall of that year, it can be regarded only as a guess. But as his estimates are nearly all high, 500,000,000 is perhaps high enough for Russia. The same authority gives France 338,000,000 bushels for 1903, Germany 130,000,000, Italy 139,000,000, Spain 123,000,000, Hungary 165,000,000, India 285,000,-000 and the United States 640,000,000.

The Hungarian minister estimates the 1903 wheat crop of the world at 3,022,000,000 bushels, which, if correct, is the greatest production of wheat the world has ever seen.

The wheat crop of the world for a series of years is estimated as follows, in round numbers:

Year	Bushels	Year	Bushels
1903	3,000,000,000	1895	2,445,000,000
1902	2,990,000,000	1894	2,555,000,000
1901	2,850,000,000	1893	2,435,000,000
1900	2,585,000,000	1892	2,340,000,000
1899	2,700,000,000	1891	2,310,000,000
1898	2,895,000,000	1890	2,225,000,000
1897	2,225,000,000	1889	2,070,000.000
1896	2,390,000,000	1888	2,150,000,000

CROP AND PRICES.

The size of the crop at once suggests an inquiry regarding the price in Chicago. The foregoing figures show an increase of nearly a billion bushels in the world's wheat crop in the last fifteen years. Referring to the record of prices from

1888 to 1891, it is found that cash wheat in Chicago in 1888 sold at 76 to 85c from Jan. 1 to July 31, advanced to 94⅜ cents by Aug. 31, and $2 on Sept. 30. This, however, was due to a corner. The rest of the year, except for a time in December, it ranged above $1.

In 1889, cash wheat ranged from $1.06¼, in March, to 75½c in June, and averaged about 80c the rest of the year.

In 1890, the range was 74½c to $1.08¼. In 1891, 85c was low point, and $1.13 high.

A glance at the wheat crops of this country shows them to have been 416,000,000 bushels in 1888; 490,000,000 in 1889; 400,000,000 in 1890, and 611,000,000 in 1891. Yet the highest average price was in 1891, and the world's crop was increasing. The crop of 1891, 611,000,000 bushels, was the record crop of this country up to 1898.

There are other factors that must be considered in connection with the size of the world's crop. One of these is distribution. Other cereals also have an important bearing on wheat prices.

The world raised, in 1902 and again in 1903, according to the Hungarian estimator, a grand total of approximately nine billion bushels of rye, barley, oats and corn, or one and one-half billion more than in the two preceding years, and one and three-fourth billion more than in 1899. A heavy shortage in these grains would offset some increase in the total wheat crop, and some decrease in wheat would be equalized by an increase in the other cereals. The effect would be greater or less according to the distribution of the crops and the amount carried over from the preceding year.

CONSUMPTION INCREASING.

In 1902 and again in 1903, as shown in the foregoing, the world's crops, all cereals, were larger than for the three years preceding. But it is worthy of particular note that the world's visible decreased in those two years, while in America, with its two good crops, of 670,000,000 and 640,000,000 bushels, respectively, the visible supply all through 1903 was much smaller than in 1902. As there was no reason to believe an unusual amount was held back by the farmers, though such might have been the case, it seems to suggest that America's consumption of wheat has greatly increased during the last ten years. In fact, if this were not so, prices should have ruled very low in those two years. Still, it is also possible, and it seems reasonable to suppose, that the world's cereal crops of 1903-'02 were largely overestimated.

The yearly consumption of wheat in the form of flour in this country has until recently been estimated at 5.20 bushels per capita. But the extensive use of "breakfast foods," which has increased rapidly in the last ten years, has considerably increased the actual consumption of wheat. The Department of Commerce, created in 1903, estimates the domestic requirements of wheat for all purposes at 6½ bushels, which makes 520,000,000 bushels required for home consumption.

THE EXPORTABLE SURPLUS OF THE UNITED STATES.

In estimating the exportable surplus of a crop, the items to be considered, are (1) the size of the crop, (2) amount carried over from the last crop, (3) amount to be carried into the next crop year, (4) consumption, and (5) reserved for seed. The remainder will be the amount that can be spared for export. Except under unusual conditions, the amount carried from one crop into the next is approximately the same; yet after a year of very low prices, there will be a much greater amount held by farmers than after a year of high prices.

As the exportable surplus of our crop is of the greatest possible importance, owing to its influence on prices throughout the year, the one item. besides the size of the crop itself, that regulates the surplus, hardly receives the attention it should; that is, the consumption. It is, in fact, of importance enough to warrant some special investigation by the agricultural department, not through its regular channels of information, but by recognized experts in that line of work. Fifty million bushels more or less for export on any crop, might mean a difference of 5 to 10 cents per bushel to the farmer on the whole crop. Considering the crop of 1903, the great importance of approximate accuracy in estimating the consumption is seen.

For comparison, the exports of wheat—corn is also given for reference—from the United States is given here, for a series of years ending June 30, as reported by the department of agriculture:

Year ending June 30	Wheat and Flour Bushels	Corn Bushels	Year ending June 30	Wheat and Flour Bushels	Corn Bushels
1881	185,000,000	92,000,000	1892	225,665,000	75,451,000
1882	122,598,000	43,000,000	1893	191,912,000	46,034,000
1883	148,785,000	41,000,000	1894	164,273,000	65,324,000
1884	111,534,000	45,000,000	1895	144,812,000	27,691,000
1885	132,570,000	51,834,000	1996	126,443,000	99,992,000
1886	94,565,000	63,655,000	1897	145,122,000	176,916.000
1887	153,804,000	40,307,000	1898	217,306,000	208,745,000
1888	119,625,000	24,278,000	1899	222,691,000	174,089,000
1889	88,600,000	69,592,000	1900	186,090,000	209,348,000
1890	109,430,000	101,973,000	1901	215,990,000	177,818,000
1891	106,181,000	30,768,000	1902	234,772,000	26,636,000

By this table it is seen that not since 1891 have the actual exports of wheat and flour fallen below 125,000,000 bushels, while in 1903 they were 235,-000,000 bushels. When the estimated exportable surplus gets down to only a little over 100,000,000 bushels, it is a matter of the utmost importance to the country that the basis for estimating is as reliable as possible.

HARVEST TIME OF THE WORLD.

The distribution of the wheat-growing countries of the world, some of them north of the equator and others south, seems a wise provision of nature; yet it benefits the European buyers more directly than any one else, and nature should not discriminate. It is, therefore, no wonder, perhaps, that the importer often asserts his influence in the market as if he were specially provided for by providence.

But to return to the harvest time of the world, it is readily seen that if India, Australia and Argentina harvested their wheat in the summer, when America and Europe do, the price during the crop movement would be depressed to an exceedingly low figure. As it is, with the Argentine harvest coming in December, the Australian in January, and the Indian in March and April, the movement of wheat is well distributed. With the increase of the Argentine crop, the tendency of prices will be toward narrower annual fluctuations, though the average may not change. The range of prices for the year, from low point to high, seems likely to be lessened also by better and quicker transportation facilities the world over.

May is the month that starts the American harvest in Texas. As soon as the click of the binders is heard, the bears prick up their ears, and lose no time in beginning to hammer the market, if conditions are at all favorable. There is no great wheat area harvested in May. Northern Africa, except Egypt, central Asia, China and Japan harvest in this month.

June is an important month. Missouri, Kansas, Oklahoma, the southern states and California; also Italy, Spain and southern France are in the midst of harvest in June.

July is the most extensive harvest month. Minnesota and the Dakotas begin cutting in July, also Washington, Oregon, Nebraska, Iowa, the central and the New England states and eastern Canada. Other countries to harvest in July are, Roumania, Bulgaria, Austria-Hungary, southern Russia, Germany, France and the south of England.

August finishes the harvest in North Dakota and northern Minnesota, Manitoba and the Northwest Territories harvest in this month, also Belgium, Holland, Denmark, Poland and Great Britain.

September and October see grain cutting in Scotland, Norway, Sweden and northern Russia.

November starts the harvest south of the equator, with Peru and South Africa. A little cutting is done in Argentina, in an early year, about November 25.

December is Argentina's harvest month. Cutting is not completed until after January 1.

January—Australia, New Zealand and Chili.

February and March—East India and Upper Egypt.

April—India, Lower Egypt, Asia Minor and Mexico.

EXPORTING COUNTRIES.

The United States exports almost twice as much wheat as any other country. The exports of wheat and flour range from 125,000,000 bushels to 235,-000,000. They have not fallen below 100,000,000 since 1888. As an approximate basis, 200,000,000 may be taken as good exports on a 600,000,000 bushel crop.

Russia comes next as an exporter. In 1902 that country exported 81,000,000 bushels, on the largest crop ever raised up to that time. The greatest exports were in 1895, when they amounted to 136,000,-000 bushels. In 1898, they amounted to 129,000,000. About 100,000,000 bushels might be taken as a standard for a good crop year.

India is a country that exports "more or less." For the crop year ending May 31, 1901, the exports were but 96,000 bushels, owing to a crop failure, while in 1892, the biggest year, they were 56,-500,000. From 1883 to 1893, inclusive, the annual exports did not fall below 25,000,000 bushels. Since 1893, until 1903, they ran above 20,000,000 but twice. For a good crop year, 30,000,000 to 50,000,-000 may be taken as a basis.

Argentina is also an uncertain country, but the acreage has increased markedly there, and the exports are likely to steadily increase for some years to come, unless crop failures interfere.

The acreage, total crop and the exports for a series of years have been as follows—the acreage compared with the crop shows the great irregularity:

Crop Year	Acreage	Yield, Bushels	Export Surplus
1903	*11,700,000	....	95,000,000
1902	9,075,000	†117,000,000	68,000,000
1901	8,140,000	56,000,000	19,500,000
1900	8,348,000	72,000,000	31,100,000
1899	7,900,000	102,000,000	72,500,000
1898	7,500,000	108,000,000	63,000,000
1897	5,880,000	50,000,000	23,700,000
1896	5,800,000	40,000,000	3,700,000
1895	5,500,000	44,000,000	19,200,000

*Early estimate; actual acreage may not have been over 10,000,000. The crop was variously estimated at from 112,000,000 to 140,000,000 bushels. Some conservative men estimated it at only 15 per cent over the 1902 crop.
†Probably overestimated 16,000,000 bushels.

Australia is not a large exporter. The greatest exports were in 1901, when Australia and New Zealand together shipped 20,800,000 bushels. The

1904 crop promises to be the greatest in the history of the country.

IMPORTING COUNTRIES.

The importing countries are, owing to their steady buying, continually influencing the market. Therefore their "requirements," an item that is estimated at the beginning of every crop year, is something to be watched.

The United Kingdom is the largest importer, taking annually since 1893 approximately 180,000,-000 bushels of wheat and flour as wheat. Of this amount 100,000,000 to 120,000,000 per year has been drawn from the United States since 1893.

Germany imports from 50,000,000 to 80,000,000 bushels of wheat annually.

Holland imports from 50,000,000 to nearly 70,-000,000 bushels of wheat annually. Belgium from 50,000,000 to 60,000,000 bushels.

Italy is an importer to the extent of 15,000,000 to 40,000,000 bushels.

France has for the last four years imported from 25,000,000 to 30,000,000 bushels annually.

Spain, Austria-Hungary, Norway, Sweden and Switzerland are importers to the extent of 5,000,000 to 15,000,000 bushels each.

THE CANADIAN NORTHWEST.

In 1902 the Canadian Northwest promised soon to become one of the great wheat-growing countries of the world. In that year Manitoba and the Northwest Territories produced 64,000,000 bushels of wheat. In 1903 the acreage was increased about

20 per cent, and a 75,000,000 bushel crop was freely predicted in the spring. There was 50,000,000 bushels harvested, and of that amount but a small percentage was No. 1. This tells the story up to this time—that the far Northwest has not yet proved itself. In time it may become all that has been predicted, and raise 250,000,000 bushels yearly, but for the present it must be classed as "uncertain." Manitoba, however, may always be relied upon for a fair, and usually for a good, crop.

MINNEAPOLIS AND THE NORTHWEST.

Minnesota and the Dakotas, by reason of their wheat crop and their mills, occupy a position, in relation to the markets of the world, as important as that of any other entire country. This is due, not to the amount of wheat raised, but to the quality. The only other source of supply of similar wheat is the Canadian Northwest. The United Kingdom wants either the wheat or the flour made from the wheat of Minnesota and the Dakotas. The result is that flour from Northwestern wheat equal to some 25,000,000 bushels of wheat is annually exported, besides a large amount of wheat. The latter goes down the lakes from Duluth.

Owing to the remarkable demand for this wheat, the question of the size of each crop of the three states is one of great importance; and for several years past, there has been a great difference of opinion regarding the crops. As a basis, 180,000,000 bushels may be taken as a full crop for the three states.

For the last seven years, the crops have been approximately as follows:

Date	Minnesota	N. Dakota	S. Dakota	Total
1903	63,000,000	45,000,000	40,000,000	148,000,000
1902	82,000,000	55,000,000	42,000,000	179,000,060
1901	80,000,000	59,000,000	52,000,000	191,000,000
1900	80,000,000	24,000,000	36,000,000	140,000,000
1899	68,000,000	52,000,000	38,000,000	158,000,000
1898	78,000,000	56,000,000	42,000,000	176,000,000
1897	60,000,000	28,000,000	21,000,000	109,000,000

So greatly has the milling capacity of the Northwest been increased, that an average crop no longer meets the requirements of the mills.

In September, 1902, the writer made an estimate of the amount of wheat actually required by the mills. This estimate was based on replies from a large number of mills, to an inquiry as to how much wheat was actually used in the crop year ending August 31 of that year. It should be remembered that the mills often shut down, or run part time, for lack of wheat. Therefore the amount required may not be what they actually grind. Neither does it represent the full milling capacity.

The estimate referred to was that the mills of the three states, including Minneapolis and Duluth, require 140,000,000 bushels of wheat annually. They will grind that much if they can get it. More recent estimates correspond very closely to this. Minneapolis grinds approximately 68,000,000 bushels; Duluth, 8,000,000; rest of Minnesota, 50,000,-000, and the Dakotas, 14,000,000. The milling and shipping demand therefore calls for a crop of not less than 200,000,000 bushels.

The daily capacity of the mills is as follows: Minneapolis, 70,000 barrels; Duluth, 8,000, rest of Minnesota, 60,000, and the Dakotas, 20,000.

When the Minneapolis mills are all running, though not grinding to their utmost capacity, they use 1¼ million bushels of wheat per week.

The heaviest week's output of the Minneapolis mills was in the week ending November 27, 1903. The amount was 454,150 barrels. The heaviest period of running, and the previous high record for a week's run, was in October and November of 1902. Five weeks continuous running resulted as follows:

Week Ending	Barrels.
October 11	443.800
October 18	427,000
October 25	431,700
November 1	426,600
November 8	448,700

The flour sales and the running of the mills are watched closely by the trade, also the buying of wheat by the mills. The latter has the more decided effect on the market. The effect of the running of the mills, whether heavy or light, is purely sentimental. Sometimes it is entirely disregarded, while at others, it is made much of. But the actual buying of cash wheat by the mills, or the lack of it, is a factor that is real. There is no sentiment about that.

WHEAT IN STORE AT MINNEAPOLIS AND DULUTH.

	MINNEAPOLIS			DULUTH		
	1903	1902	1901	1903	1902	1901
Jan. 1.....	14,000,000	15,255,000	16,000,000	3,600,000	9,340,000	6,000,000
Feb 1.....	15,145,000	16,913,000	17,100,000	4,000,000	10,460,000	7,000,000
Mch 1.....	15,350,000	15,966,000	17,100,000	5,590,000	12,349,000	7,600,000
April 1....	13,750,000	13,800,000	16,600,000	6,420,000	14,400,000	9,200,000
May 1.....	11,000,000	9,850,000	14,500,000	4,120,000	10,800,000	10,100,000
June 1.....	6,900,000	6,400,000	12,120,000	2,180,000	7,600,000	5,463,000
July 1.....	5,200,000	5,690,000	10,500,000	1,570,000	4,500,000	3,600,000
Aug. 1.....	2,815,000	4,750,000	7,000,000	285,000	2,300,000	1,800,000
Sept.1.....	887,000	1,725,000	4,500,000	165,000	400,000	1,300,000
Oct. 1.....	3,000,000	1,300,000	6,300,000	1,000,000	1,480,000	4,700,000
Nov. 1.....	3,850,000	5,057,000	9,300,000	250,000	2,356,000	5,300,000
Dec. 1.....	7,000,000	8,000,000	13,300,000	1,250,000	3,250,000	6,200,000

CHAPTER V.

CROP REPORTS.

There are two systems of crop reporting employed in this country, namely, that of the government, which is a summary of a large number of reports, and that of individuals, some of which are based on personal inspection of the area reported on. The department of agriculture issues a report on the 10th of each month, at 3 o'clock. These reports cover all kinds of farm products in all the states. The individual reports cover wheat and corn only, and some of them spring wheat, or the Kansas crop, only.

Five of the government reports, those of April, May, July, August and September, are principally on the condition of wheat, besides fruit and other products that are of no interest to the trade. The most important reports are issued in March, July and December.

January and February reports are on miscellaneous crops.

March reports give an estimate on the supplies of wheat, corn and oats in farmers' hands—this is the larger part of the "invisible supply." Also an estimate is given on the quality of the crops and on the total wheat crop of the world.

April reports give the condition of winter wheat.

May reports are on condition of winter wheat, spring plowing, cotton area and planting.

June reports are on condition of spring and winter wheat, oats and cotton.

July reports give the acreage and condition of corn, average condition of spring and winter wheat, average condition of oats. Also, the amount of wheat in farmers' hands is estimated.

August reports give the average condition of spring wheat, corn, oats and cotton. Also, the quantity of oats in farmers' hands.

September reports are on the condition of winter wheat, corn, cotton and of oats when harvested.

October reports estimate the average yield per acre of wheat and oats, and give the condition of corn and cotton.

November reports give the yields of corn and cotton, with comparisons with the previous year.

Two reports are issued in December. That of the 10th gives the acreage sown to winter wheat and the condition of the growing crop. A report later in the month is an estimate of the total of the crop harvested the preceding summer.

THE NORTHWESTERN CROP.

Reports of individual estimators are issued but once or twice a year. The most important of these, in its effect on the markets, are those on the crop of the Northwest—Minnesota and the Dakotas. Owing to the fact that, for two years past, the mills have been unable to get sufficient wheat during the summer, the estimates of the Northwestern crop have been discussed to an unusual degree. Yet the actual number of bushels raised is of less importance than the relative size of the crop. The milling and shipping requirements of the Northwest are well known. Therefore, if it is generally conceded that the 1903 crop, for instance, was some 30,000,000 bushels smaller than the 1902, it really does not matter whether the crop was 150,000,000 or 200,-000,000. If the latter figures are right, then the 1902 crop was some 230,000,000 bushels, whereas, if the former figures are correct, the 1902 crop was 180,000,000.

Whatever the size of the 1902 crop, which may now be taken as a basis, as it was almost entirely ground or shipped out, it must be conceded that a smaller crop is insufficient for milling and shipping demands; and this is more important than the probable number of bushels raised. The relative size of a crop is also easier to estimate. Those who travel over the country every summer to look at the crops, can form a fair idea of the size, as compared with the previous crop. Yet few indeed can make an estimate in bushels that will stand the test of the threshing returns.

While the estimates, in bushels, of the 1903 crop differ by about 50,000,000, there is no difference of opinion regarding a probable shortage of supplies during the summer of 1904. Conditions have changed so rapidly in the last half dozen years that crops previous to 1902 cannot be taken as a standard of size. But henceforth, until new factors come into the general situation, that crop can be used as a basis for estimates. Any crop smaller will certainly not supply the demands of the mills and the shippers, and a crop 10 per cent larger would not be a

large crop, judged by the increased milling demand
for spring wheat.

The most exhaustive individual reports on the
Northwest crops are issued by H. V. Jones. Mr.
Jones personally inspects a large area every summer,
and as he has done this for the last fourteen years,
he can readily detect any crop diversification in any
locality. Then, too, he walks into the fields and inspects the growing grain, and he also has records of
the actual yield of certain fields for a series of years.
His is a perfect system, backed by an intuitive
ability to estimate the yield of a field of wheat.

The Jones estimates for the three states for the
last three years follow:

	1903 Acres	1902 Acres	1901 Acres
Minnesota	5,200,000	5,960,000	6,250,000
North Dakota	4,100,000	3,950,000	5,200,000
South Dakota..........	3,300,000	3,500,000	• 3,000,000
Total.............	12,600,000	13,410,000	14,450,000

	1903 Bushels	Per Acre	1902 Bushels	Per Acre	1901 Bushels	Per Acre
Minnesota.	62,400,000	12	82,150,000	13.7	78,000,000	12.5
North Dak.	45,100,000	11	55,100,000	14	75,000,000	14.5
SouthDak.	39,600,000	12	41,600,000	11.8	30,000,000	10.
Total....	147,100,000	11.66	178,850,000	13.1	183,000,000	12.3

MARKET INFLUENCE OF CROP REPORTS.

The more important of the government reports
are awaited with great interest by the trade. It
often happens that the market on the 10th will be
narrow and uneventful, awaiting the report, which
is not issued until 3 p. m. For a week in the first
part of August, 1903, the market was narrow, as the

trade was disinclined to make any aggressive move until the Jones estimate on the Northwestern crop had been issued. This came out on the morning of the 10th, and the government report in the afternoon. As soon as these reports were "out of the way," a drag seemed to have been removed from the market, and trade went on with renewed activity.

It sometimes happens that reports are "discounted" before they are issued. The trade, by following conditions, forms an impression of what it will be, bullish or bearish, and anticipates it by putting the market up or down before the report is given out. In such an event, the market may decline on a bullish report or advance on a bearish one. It not infrequently happens that the market takes this contrary course on the 11th. For instance, it may advance on the 10th and be very strong at the close. Then, if the report at 3 o'clock is conceded to be bullish, it seems reasonable to expect an advance the following day. Yet "the crowd" all seem to have a little wheat to sell on the 11th, evidently taking advantage of the "hard spot" to "dump" it. The market is almost sure to close lower in such cases. On bearish reports, these conditions are of course reversed.

It sometimes happens that a report is so radical that no one gives it credence. This was the case with the Jones report of August 10th, 1903. Chicago was bearish at that time, and had discounted a fairly bullish report, as they expected his and the government reports would be. Taken by surprise, therefore, by figures smaller than any one had expected, Chicago simply refused to accept them.

CHAPTER VI.

ERRORS THAT ARE EASILY MADE.

As pointed out in a preceding chapter, the first, or primary, error made in speculating, and the one that leads to many secondary errors, is in people thinking they can make money at speculation before they have learned the business; in fact, before they have any conception of what is to be learned. The writer feels safe in asserting positively that no man ever became a successful trader without long study and experience, and many disappointments. No one can expect to deal successfully in cash grain without serving a tiresome apprenticeship. Yet the "undertone" of the market is infinitely more difficult to read than a handful of wheat or corn. The latter is a mechanical proposition, to a large extent. Reading the tone of the market requires an intuitive perception that cannot be taught nor learned. If it is in a man, it may be developed. If a man does not possess it, the sooner he finds it out, the better off and happier he will be.

The foregoing statements require some qualification when a distinction is made between the speculator and the investment buyer, or seller. The chief qualification of the man who wishes to invest in grain or stocks for a "long pull" and a big profit, is patience, following, of course, some knowledge of what he is about.

The first error then, is ignorance; and the second, the writer believes, should be credited to obstinacy. The obstinate man is sure—absolutely certain—to take some big losses unless he has unlimited capital to back up his "bull-headedness." It is useless to "think" the market will not do this or that. Your "thinking" will not change the trend of the market, so when you discover that you have thought wrong, it is usually wise to get out as quickly and cheaply as possible. This is easy advice, but difficult of enactment.

There is also another phase of obstinacy. That is, in refusing to see but one side to the market; in other words, in always being either a bull or a bear. If a man is so constituted that he cannot be a bear, he owes it to his heirs to keep out of the market, when it persistently goes against him, until it touches bottom. It is discouraging to be a bull all the way down a 10c decline, or to be a bear all the way up a 15c advance. Obstinacy is a heavy handicap to some men who would otherwise be eminently successful in the speculative field.

It is not always obstinacy, however, that causes one often to take a big loss. One frequently hears the remarks, "Take a small loss, but let your profits run;" "never take a loss after you have had a profit;" "never take over ½c or 1c loss," etc. These things sound easy, yet they are only applicable to the scalper. While a man should place a limit on the amount of money he will invest, or risk, on a transaction, it may not be advisable to limit the loss on each trade; as, for example, he may buy a small amount at a certain price, intending to take a little more on a cent decline, etc. When he has thus accumulated his "line," if he is a conservative man and not one of the obstinate kind, he will place a stop-loss order a little below the last purchase price.

It is wonderfully easy to let a loss run, yet equally hard to wait patiently for a small profit to increase. It seems to be human nature to hope for the best when a loss is growing bigger, yet to snatch eagerly at a small profit for fear it will get away.

One of the common mistakes of most speculators, and which seems to be another trait of human nature, is in thinking one has made a profit before the trade is actually closed, if the transaction goes in his favor. That is, if one has a profit in sight, he thinks he is losing money if the market begins to go the other way. This leads to the error of often taking a loss after one has a profit, for the trader is reluctant to take less profit than he could have had at one time. Therefore he waits, hoping the market will go back again. It may, but as likely it will wipe out the remaining profit; and then the man will not close the trade even, but may finally have to take a loss.

It often happens that the market goes against one immediately after a trade is made. One buys at 75c, say, and the market declines to 74c. Then it works back to 75c, and seems strong; so strong, in fact, that the trader concludes to hold the purchase. This may be good judgment, and again it may not. The question to ask one's self is, If I didn't have this trade, would I buy now, after a cent advance? Conditions will not always be the same. It may be a scalping market, an advancing or a declining market; and you have practically purchased on a "bulge." Look at it from this view point and decide for yourself; do not say to some one else, "What do you think of the market?" The question of "buying on bulges" deserves some consideration, but this will be reserved for the next chapter.

A common mistake is to "get in and out of the market" frequently without having a strong conviction either way as to whether there are good reasons why the price should advance or decline. In discussing this point with the writer, an old broker gave it as his observation that this is the cause of many mistakes on the part of traders. Some man may watch the market for a time, cautiously and hesitatingly, and study both sides. Having thus arrived at a state of conviction, he makes a trade, and possibly is successful. Then he becomes eager to get into the market again. He cannot wait so patiently the next time; and the result is that he is soon in and out almost every day. He soon loses all judgment and merely "thinks" the market is going one way or the other, without having any well-grounded reasons.

Now here is a very pretty distinction between the green, untrained trader and the man of experience who has had his judgment, and his nerves, too, tried in many a puzzling market. The untrained man believes the market will advance or decline—that is, he "feels" that it will. So he risks his money on

sensation, a sentiment, which may only have been
suggested by something he overheard or read. The
man of experience, however, may often trade on
impulse or his feeling regarding the market, because he has found that he can intuitively read the
undertone. He may not be able to say why he is
bullish or bearish, but only that the market acts,
"feels," as if it were going to advance or decline. He
has learned that his instinctive feeling can be followed, to a certain extent. This, of course, is impossible for the new trader.

An error sometimes made even by experienced
traders, is to buy on a break without first waiting
for the market to steady itself. For example, the
market advances from 75c to 8oc, say, then begins
to break. Some bull, who expects a 10c advance,
thinks this a good chance to get in; so he places an
order to buy at 79c. Another thinks that if it goes
back to 78c, it will be cheap, so he places an order
at that figure. Yet what they thought to be only a
little reaction proves to be a wicked shake-out or a
discouraging slump, and the price goes back possibly 4c before it begins to steady itself. The more
conservative trader will wait patiently until the nature of the decline has manifested itself. This feature of the market will also be touched upon in the
succeeding chapter.

Under the head of errors, it seems hardly necessary to mention that of taking larger trades, assum-
ing greater risks, than the trader's capital justifies.
The larger the transaction, in proportion to one's
capital, the more careful one should be to stop the

loss, if the trade goes against one, before it becomes large. The matter of limiting one's loss is of vital importance, and the further the market is from a conservative price basis, the more watchful the trader must be to stop his losses.

CHAPTER VII.

SOME SUGGESTIONS TO TRADERS AND ON TRADING.

This chapter is begun with much of the feeling suggested by a certain writer who advised his followers to work out their own salvation "with fear and trembling." This advice seems, after thoughtful consideration of it, to apply equally as well to speculation as to salvation. If one begins with fear and trembling, he is less likely to have it to do on a larger scale later on. The words suggest conservatism; though if carried to an extreme, they might mean "weak-kneed," or lack of courage. The man who lacks in courage will never be much of a figure in the market. While he may at times be successful in a small way, he lacks the qualities that are absolutely necessary for the trader. Besides courage, the ability to decide questions while others are thinking about them, is of vital importance; and added to this is conservatism. If a man lacks in boldness and conservatism, he had better keep out of the market, for he will be continually tormented with doubts, and will buy when he should have sold, and sell when he should buy. He will trade in "2's" on a real bull market, because of lack of courage; and then, seeing how much he might have made, he will lose his head and buy a "10" at the top of the bulge. The market is no place for such a man, any more than for the obstinate man.

Perhaps one of the best suggestions that can be given the man who has designs on the market, is that he first take himself in hand. Let him analyze himself, sorting out the strong points and the weak ones, not sparing his vanity in the operation. Finding where he is weak, he may avoid many errors, and possibly develop the qualities that he desires. Judgment, however, is a hard thing to develop, unless one has a good foundation to work upon.

DEPEND UPON YOUR OWN JUDGMENT.

A common weakness found among inexperienced traders is the lack of confidence in one's own judgment. Another, is to become prejudiced as soon as one's mind is made up. Some men then become obstinate. Depending on one's judgment to the extent of obstinacy when events are proving one wrong, is a serious mistake. Some traders will pay no attention to news or opinions contrary to their convictions. They will ask others for their opinion, hoping that it will coincide with their own. This paragraph might fittingly have found a place in the preceding chapter, under the head of "Errors," but that it is desired to offer a suggestion on this point.

The matter of asking opinions on the market is one which has been given a great deal of thought by the writer. As a general proposition, he believes it worse than useless, for the reason that the inquirer can seldom know how the one asked arrived at his conclusions nor whether his judgment is biased. Then, too, some men are always bulls, and others always bears. An opinion from either of this class may cheer or depress one's spirits for the time, but it would do neither if he knew the one asked always felt the same. If the market is strong, or weak, you can detect it as well as anyone. It is always strongest on the bulges, and weakest on the slumps. These are the points to be watched, for no one can tell you what will happen at such times.

Where the inexperienced may, and should, profit by the observations and knowledge of the experienced, however, is in gathering from them the important facts that go to make up the prevailing situation. Then one should himself digest these facts and arrive at his own conclusions. Learn to think for yourself.

The trader should select his broker with the same care that he does his banker. The broker should be an adviser, as far as consistent; yet the trader should be cautious lest the advice tend too much toward commissions. The broker is in such sympathetic touch with the market that he can often detect the culmination of an advance or a decline, or the spots where one should take profits, or buy or sell.

WHAT KIND OF A TRADER ARE YOU?

Temperament, or nature, divides men who trade, into two distinct classes, as different as black and white, namely, the bulls and the bears. Yet there are exceptional men who can trade on either side of the market without prejudice. Observation inclines the writer to believe that many of the mistakes made in the market are made by natural bulls trying to "play" the bear side, or vice-versa. Such an undertaking is much like that of a Northern man trying to live in the tropics—nature did not design him for it, and he can never be quite at home there.

Probably the reason that most traders can be successful on but one side of the market, is that their prejudices prevent their reasoning correctly when out of their element. An important question for the inexperienced trader to settle, therefore, is, whether he is naturally a bull, or bear. Having once established this in his mind, he may be saved many losses through restraining his natural tendencies under certain conditions; as, for example, the bear should not allow himself to become too pessimistic when wheat is below 70c, nor the bull too confident when it is above 80c. In the former case, let the bear reason something like this: "I'm a bear by nature, therefore the price never looks too low. Yet there may be another side that I cannot see, so I'll be cautious." Then, at times, when wheat is above 80c, the bull might profitably reason thus: "Although I know that legitimate conditions warrant 90c for wheat, I am a bull and therefore may be prejudiced. Perhaps I don't read the indications aright. I'll walk around the pasture a bit and look at the scenery. Maybe the market will appear differently when I get back." It is a wise bull or a wise bear that can try to see the market with the other's eyes.

The man that can play a bull market up, and then turn around and play a bear market down to the starting point again, is designed by nature for a trader. He would be out of his element in any other field.

When a man discovers to which class he belongs,

he will be more than ordinarily cautious when he ventures on the opposite side for a turn.

Traders are again divided into those who are by temperament scalpers and those whose tendency is more toward the investment order of trading. Some men are restless from the time they make a trade until it is closed. Others will make a purchase or a short sale and forget it for weeks. The former are numerous, and the latter compose a small majority. The following is an extreme case, yet it actually happened: During the big advance in 1896, a broker had an order from a farmer in North Dakota to buy 5,000 bushels of wheat. The order was executed, and although the price advanced several cents, nothing further was heard from the farmer. Bulges and slumps came and went, though the trend was upward, and the weeks passed into months, yet the account was unclosed. Finally the broker wrote to the farmer, suggesting that as he had a big profit, it would be good business to take it. No reply. Several more weeks passed, when, one day, the broker had a letter from Sweden, where the farmer had gone on a visit, saying that as wheat had had a good advance, to close the trade and send him a draft for the balance.

The opposite of this man is he who stands in the pit and buys and sells at the same price if the market does not at once go his way, or who takes a 1-16 less or ⅛ profit—who will never take a greater loss than ⅛ if he can help it, and never tries for a greater profit than ⅜, and seldom carries a trade over night.

Now these two classes of traders did not make themselves that way; nature did it, and the men follow their natural tendencies. One could not play the other's game.

Every man has a natural tendency toward one or the other of the two extremes—the scalper or the investment buyer. The easiest and most natural method of trading is the one the trader should cultivate—the one that he can follow with the least strain upon himself.

An error of the inexperienced is to imitate some successful trader. This frequently results in a bull playing understudy to a bear, or a scalper to a natural investment buyer. To again quote the writer referred to at the beginning of this chapter, "work out your own salvation." Find out where you belong, and then develop the best that is in you.

BUYING ON BULGES—RUN-AWAY MARKETS INFRE-
QUENT.

Beware of the excitement of sharp advances, is a suggestion worthy of consideration. There is something exhilarating about an advancing market. Every one is affected to some extent, unless they are on the short side. Right at the climax of the bulge, it seems so strong that even old traders can scarcely resist buying. The market often closes that way; but in the morning it is "all gone." There are no buyers, but everyone has a little to sell. This transformation is incomprehensible to "outsiders." The experienced trader knows that every little flurry does not portend a bull market. Big advances and declines come but two or three times a year, therefore do not expect one every week.

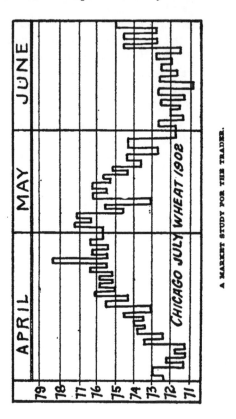

There is nothing more discouraging nor yet more common than buying on bulges. One should learn to buy on the weak spots and to sell on the hard ones—a difficult proposition, by the way, easy as it seems. Buying when the market is strong (there are exceptional times, as on a real bull market) often results in the trader getting loaded up, so that he cannot take advantage of weak and lower places that usually follow the bulges. The trader will often thus be tied up until he becomes thoroughly disgusted, and finally closes the trade out just at the wrong time.

One may profitably resolve never to buy after an advance of 3c without a reaction of at least a cent. This applies to short selling as well—do not get bearish and sell short after a 3c break (of course exactly 3c is not meant, but "about" 3c) which has come without a reaction of a cent. Perhaps twice a year one will miss an opportunity by adhering to this resolve, for big slumps and run-away markets sometimes come without reactions. For example, May corn broke from the high point of the fall of 1903, which was 52⅞c, the middle of September, down to 47⅛c with but one reaction of ½c. Here was a break of 5¾c with but one reaction of ½c. At the same time, Chicago December wheat broke exactly 7c without a reaction of a cent. There were two reactions of ¾c each. Yet in the whole December option, from June 1 to December 1, this is the only time one would have missed it by waiting for the reaction after about a 3c advance or decline.

Of course, it does not follow that after an advance or decline of 3c followed by a reaction, wheat or other grains should be bought or sold. That, of course, depends on the kind of market, and the movement before the sharp advance or decline.

WHEN TO BUY AND WHEN TO SELL.

Theoretically, there are two distinct times to buy and to sell short, namely, when the market is extremely weak or very strong.

It may sound like strange council to so say that one should both buy and sell when the market is weak, and again to both buy and sell when the market is strong. Yet this is exactly the meaning of the preceding paragraph. But there is "real" strength and "seeming" strength, and "actual" weakness and "seeming" weakness. These differences the trader, to be successful, must learn to distinguish. These conditions arise somewhat as follows: During a slowly but steadily advancing market there will be numerous reactions of from 1c to 3c. After an advance of, say, 3c without a reaction of over ½c, there is likely to be a quick break of 1 to 1½ c. At the bottom of such breaks, the market is often slow to recover, and seems very weak. Yet this is just the time for the bull to look to his courage, take stock of conditions again, and, if he still believes he is right, fearlessly buy as much on this weak spot as his trading capital and the general price warrant. This is buying when the market seems very weak, but when, in reality, the legitimate conditions are strong and the price is not inconsistent with the conditions.

Just before the little break, the market seemed exceedingly strong, yet the experienced trader who was also a good reader of the undertone, saw on that "hard spot" a good place to take profits. He took profits on his long stuff, and, if he was an all-'round trader, he sold a little short for a quick turn.

Buying when the market is strong requires less courage but more judgment than buying on the "soft" places. Yet on a real "old-fashioned" bull market, any one can jump in and buy and make money—for a time. A broker with a large business told the writer that on the big advance during the "Leiter deal," all his customers made money; but they all lost it again on the decline. They could not play both sides of the market.

As big advances without numerous reactions seldom come, it is not often necessary for one to buy when the market really acts the strongest. By waiting, one can, nine times out of ten, buy at a little lower price. Yet occasionally the market will develop such strength that it would be foolish to wait for a reaction. Examples will be given in the chapter on charts.

The places to sell short are the reverse of those to buy. On the hard spots of advancing markets, after advances of from 2c to 3c, the bears usually feel safe in putting out a line. Yet they are often deceived by the seeming, not actual, weakness which follows, and by overselling, help to cause a quick reaction. The bear is a courageous beast, but his habit of always looking down leads him into many a scrape, and he is often forced to take to the woods with the bulls in hot pursuit.

Only the all-'round trader or the natural bear has the courage to sell short on the hard spots of an ad-

vancing market. The bull may take his profits on
the advances, but he waits for a reaction to buy in
again. A pig on the ice is a graceful creature compared with the real bull on the short side of the
market. He cannot become enthusiastic in that position.

After an advance of 10c or more, it often happens
that a decline as great will follow. Such markets are
the joy of the bear. He sells short on the first weakness, keeps selling as the market grows softer and develops into a slump, takes his profit when it begins to
show resistance, puts out new lines on the reactions
of ¾ to 1c, and slugs and hammers and pounds
away in a delirium of mad, bearish joy that is incomprehensible to the bull, who stands sadly by
watching the ruin.

Selling during the slumps of a real bear market
following a long advance, is as easy and natural to
the bear, and as prolific of profits, as is buying on a
legitimate bull market to the bull. When a market
really begins to slide off, it goes as easily as a to-
boggan down hill. At such times it is permissible
to sell when it is weak.

ABOUT TAKING PROFITS.

Half of the successful trader's art lies in his ability to save his profits after he has made them. Few
traders, unless they are scalpers in the pit, get all the
profit they might, while most of them get a full
measure of loss when the market goes against them.
The investment buyer, or seller, saves a much larger percentage of a profit than the man who takes
small profits. On a 3c advance, a keen trader may

get a profit of 2½c. The inexperienced trader will come out of it something like this: To start with, he will not have the courage to buy at the bottom, and the market will get away from him ¾c before he gets in. Then, at the top of the advance, it will seem so strong he will not take his profit. A break of 1c, say, follows, and the market looks weak; so the trader closes out to save what profit there is left. He has lost ¾c at one end and 1c at the other. This from 3c leaves him 1¼c profit on a 3c advance. Better than a loss, of course; yet it leaves something to be desired. Until he can secure a larger percentage of profit than this, he can hardly call himself an expert trader. Perhaps he never will become one. Thousands are trying to, but cannot; yet the percentage of successful traders is probably as great as the percentage of experts in other lines of business or in the professions.

When to take profits depends, of course, altogether on the kind of market it is, whether bear, bull, or merely a scalping affair, and on the trader, whether he is an investment buyer, a scalper, or one who is satisfied with moderate profits. As the great majority of non-professional traders belong to the latter class, that is the only one that needs to be considered here.

It has been shown that big advances without numerous reactions seldom come, and that after an advance of about 3c the trader should wait for a reaction of about 1c before buying. Therefore it seems to follow that after an advance of about 3c—not from the point at which he bought but from where

the advance started—the trader should unhesitatingly take his profit, and wait for a reaction to buy in
again. On less active markets, it will prove profitable, in the long run, to take profits on all fluctuations of from 1c to 2c. Yet as some traders are continually expecting either a big bull or a bear market,
moderate profits look small to them. They want it
all, and in an endeavor to get it, they frequently take
losses. A method, and a safe one, adopted by some
conservative traders when they think a big advance
likely, is, when they have a profit, to place a stop
order at about the purchase price. Then they let
the profit run, risking only that already earned.
This they are willing to risk rather than to take a
moderate profit when they believe there is the possibility of a run-away market in their favor. If the
market steadily advances, they may move their stop
order up, so that in case of a reaction they will have
some profit at least.

A careful study of the range of prices from the
beginning of any option to its close, will show that
if one had bought say 10,000 bushels near the low
point, and had carried it to near the high point, or
vice-versa, ignoring the fluctuations of 1c, 2c, or
even 5c, he would have made a handsome profit,
probably several times as much as the average trader made through frequently getting in and out. Yet
few men are so constituted that they can trade in this
way, although many resolve time after time that they
will hold for a "long pull" next time the market is
favorable.

One of the most successful traders of the writer's

acquaintance has a way of holding for a big profit and also of securing profits that would be a joy to many another trader, if the plan could be as successfully carried out. But this trader possesses unusual ability to read the undertone of the market. On

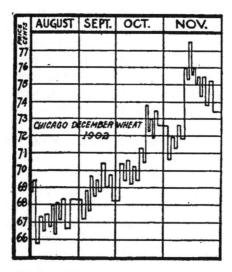

In such an advance as this, with numerous fluctuations, the trader who would scalp with half his line, ie., sell half his line on every advance and buy it back on the first decline, would make more than either the long-pull trader or the scalper.

an advancing market, for example, when he is convinced that much higher prices will ultimately rule, he will buy say 20,000 bushels on some weak place. He feels perfectly safe with this amount, and as his judgment is good as to when to buy, he is not scared out by a little decline. Now when an advance comes, say of 1½c, or as many points, if the market hesitates at all, he quickly and without any misgivings sells half his line. Then if there is a moderate reaction, he buys back as much as sold, and has his original line and a profit as well. But if the price continues to advance, he merely holds what he has, and buys again on the first reaction. In the course of a 10c advance, he has secured many profits of from ¾c to 1½c on 10 wheat and has, besides, carried the other 10 to near the top. Some traders in the stock market buy one stock as an investment and another and more active one to scalp with. Some times there are numerous fluctuations in some particular stock although the actual change in price during several weeks may be small. Also, at times, one may buy or sell corn or oats for an investment, and scalp the wheat market. Or, again, one may buy a distant grain future for an investment, and do his principal trading in the more active, nearby future.

TRADE IN THE ACTIVE FUTURES.

A suggestion that observation has shown is a valuable one to many, is that the trader should confine his transactions to the active futures, unless manipulation should make them dangerous. If May wheat is being traded in mostly, as it is from Nov. 15 to April 1, as a rule, the trader will find it decidedly to his advantage—there may be exceptions, of course—to confine his transactions to this future. The fluctuations will be greater than those of July or September, and often there may be a very active market in the near-by future while the more distant ones are quiet.

WHEN TO STOP LOSSES.

This is probably the most difficult problem in the whole range of the market that the trader has to solve. One thing he must reconcile himself to, however, and that is the taking of an occasional loss. If a loss is stopped while it is small, it cannot become big,—that is certain. It is also certain that the better a man's judgment as to buying or selling, the fewer losses he will have to face.

Most of the small losses, on the long side, are the result of buying on the hard places, just when good traders are taking profits, and waiting for a reaction to buy again. The big losses come from a mistake in judging the whole situation. The natural bear misjudges a bull market, or a bull a bear market, becomes obstinate or cannot correctly estimate the value of conditions, and so hangs on until finally forced to cover. The writer has known a trader to take a 10c loss, closing out just before the market turned and went back to the starting point.

Besides the loss itself, if one is forced to take it, the trader, by hanging on, is thereby kept from trading and possibly making some profits. In the case given, if the trader had not closed out, but had waited for the market to go back, he would only have come out even. As it was, he was kept from trading all the way down a 10c decline, and then had no confidence in his judgment, so that he did not take advantage of the 10c advance which followed.

The advantages of taking a loss are often much greater than those of making a profit. If every one's first trade or so resulted in a loss, the educational process would be laid on a better foundation than if gains were scored. Inexperienced traders, and some of fairly long experience, would do well to accept a few losses instead of trying to work their way out of them, even when the latter process seems reasonably certain, just as a sort of training and sacrifice for having got into the market wrong. Only to get out from under the shadow of a big loss by taking a small one, often changes a man's whole attitude toward the market. He can then view the situation in an unprejudiced frame of mind, and pat himself on the back for having had the courage to accept a loss. One of the oldest traders of the writer's acquaintance says that he has (after years of ups and downs, big successes and large losses) made it an absolute rule never to take over 1c loss on wheat or one point on stocks. This is a hard rule to follow, but experience has taught this trader that nothing else is safe for him.

No general rule can be laid down for stopping losses. This is another situation where every man must work out his own salvation. A man with ample capital who trades in "5's" or "10's," will not be bound by the same limitations as the trader who deals in "50's" or "100's." Yet it is also safe to say that the former trader will not display the same conservatism in buying or selling as will the latter; and this is a suggestion worthy of some study.

MARKET LETTERS, REVIEWS AND "GOSSIP."

Now that several daily, as well as some weekly, papers make a feature of publishing the market letters of brokers, the situation and conditions are given a much wider and more general circulation than when, outside the centers, people had to depend on private sources of information and the market pages of their papers. In the cities, of course, one has access to the current "gossip" that is continually being sent out by the big private wire houses of Chicago, on grain, and of New York, on the stock market.

Market letters form a valuable source of information to the trader. But in reading them, he should not permit himself to fall into the mistake of accepting the conclusions of only those that agree with himself. Unless one is careful, he is likely to find himself scoffing at opinions contrary to his own. Yet taking the successful trader as an example, and we find a man who is always open to conviction; in fact, eager to be convinced if his judgment is at fault. If he has arrived at wrong conclusions, no one needs to know it more than he; it means money to him. Therefore, such a man is always studying both sides of the situation; although to be a successful trader, he must have sufficient self reliance and reasoning power not to be influenced by plausible yet erroneous views of the market.

Sometimes those who write market letters or gossip or the market reviews of the papers may be wrong for months at a time. A notable instance of this was during the fall of 1903. Some of the Chi-

cago houses never wrote an optimistic market letter nor sent out a cheerful bit of gossip during an
advance of 9c in wheat, which covered a period of
two months. Then, too, after a decline of over 11c
in May corn, several prominent houses, in their
market letters, continually advised selling it short
at 42c. Yet it turned around and advanced 13c.

These instances are given, not in a critical spirit,
for no man can always foretell the trend of prices,
but to point out the advisability of carefully studying both sides of the market, no matter what author-
ities may be on either side. This is taking the reader back to where it is suggested that he learn to rely
upon his own judgment.

In reading market letters, one should also avoid
regarding any particular writer's opinion as worthy
of acceptance without argument. The writer of this
has systematically read market letters and market
reviews for years—made a study of them, in fact,
and has never yet found the infallible writer. Even
the best of the market writers fall down at times, and
sometimes fall exceedingly hard. When a writer
who has been on one side of the market for a considerable period, changes front and gives his reasons for the change, if he has been right so far, he
is generally a good man to follow, though cautiously. For the oftener a man is right, consecutively, in
his market prognostications, the nearer he is to the
inevitable fall-down.

The trader should not expect any market writer
to call the fluctuations—that is asking too much of
a mortal. The conservative man who studies con-

ditions carefully, however, should be able to tell the logical tendency of prices. This, it seems, should be the aim of all commercial editors and those who write market letters, and is all that any one should ask of them. Merely to write what has happened is of no use only as a matter of record—which posterity will never read.

Like speculators, commercial editors and the writers of market letters are (unfortunately and perhaps unconsciously) either bulls or bears. Their reviews are therefore likely to be influenced by the natural inclination of the man. Then, too, they are likely to become careless as to their sources of information, going too frequently to certain men for their views, for example, and so being influenced in either direction.

The careful reader of market reviews and letters should learn which are always either pessimistic or optimistic, and avoid them altogether or only glance at them. He wants both sides laid before him, and both sides carefully analyzed or left for his own analysis.

LITTLE THINGS.

Enough might be written of the minor features of the market to form a book of itself. As so much must therefore be omitted, mention will be made of but a few. It should be understood that, excepting during a very active market, most of the trading is of a professional nature That is, it is largely done by the "floor traders" and the daily patrons of the brokerage offices. This class of traders is quick to run or to take profits, which results in many of the small price fluctuations. It is a custom with the majority of them to "even up" on Saturdays or the day before a holiday, and this often causes an advance or a decline on those days. When the trend of the market is steadily upward, the close on Saturdays is likely to be rather strong. This is because the shorts are afraid to go over until Monday short of the market, and the buying in of their lines causes some advance. The contrary is the case when the general tendency of the market is downward. Again, it frequently happens that if the market closes strong on Saturday, there will be a little spurt some time on Monday, followed by a decline. The reason for this is that there are more market letters sent out on Saturday than any other day, and if the situation seems strong, they are likely to be tinged with bullishness. The result is that a larger number of buying orders than usual find their way to the pit on Monday, and these have the effect of temporarily advancing the price slightly. After these are executed, the bears, finding no more aggressive buying, begin to get busy, and hammer the price down for a scalp.

It must be understood that the foregoing is not laid down as a rule, but it occurs frequently enough so that one should be cautious about buying on a firm and slightly higher market on Mondays. It is better to take profits on long wheat on such hard spots.

To a greater or lesser extent, what is true of Saturdays and Mondays is true of the close and the opening of the market daily. If the market opens strong and immediately runs up ⅜ to ¾c, it will usually (bull or bear markets are not being considered now) work back again; and this is also true of a weak opening. One is often deceived by this "seeming" strength and is tempted to buy, or by a weak opening and is constrained to sell out long wheat. One should, therefore, unless in exceptional cases, as during a real bull or bear market, wait for 10 or 15 minutes or more after the opening, until the market "settles down," before placing new orders, unless to sell short on the advance, or to buy on a weak opening.

CHAPTER VIII.

MISCELLANEOUS MARKET FEATURES.

There are several features of the market that seem to belong under such a head as the foregoing. Foremost in importance among them is "spreading."

"SPREADING."

Theoretically, spreading is a "conservative" form of speculation; sometimes it seems almost like a sure thing, and it often proves so when the markets are governed by normal conditions. Yet when manipulation becomes a factor, spreading is exceedingly dangerous, and some of the wickedest losses ever suffered have been through spreading between different markets. This form of speculation is practiced in a scalping way as well as for a long-time investment.

The several methods of spreading are : To buy one future and to sell another in the same market, as, to buy Minneapolis May or July and sell September, or to buy July and sell May, or to buy Chicago May and sell Chicago July, etc. To buy (or sell) in Minneapolis, Duluth, St. Louis or New York, and to sell (or buy) in Chicago.

RELATIVE POSITIONS OF DIFFERENT MARKETS.

Again, theoretically, there should be a relative difference between the various markets—Chicago, Minneapolis, St. Louis, New York and Liverpool—based on the difference in freight rates. This does

not and cannot hold good, for several reasons. One
of these is that local conditions affect the individual
markets. The milling demand for wheat at Minneapolis, for instance, keeps that market more or less
out of line with Chicago continually. Then, too,
the kind of wheat deliverable on contracts in the
different markets has an important bearing on their
relative position. The rules of the Chicago Board
of Trade permit No. 1 northern, No. 2 red or No. 2
hard winter wheat, the latter at a penalty of 2c per
bushel, to be delivered on contracts. At St. Louis,
only No. 2 red is deliverable. Minneapolis rules
call for No. 1 northern only.

It is easily seen, therefore, that, with a shortage
of contract wheat in the Northwest, Minneapolis
prices might range very high without Chicago being materially affected; and that a shortage of No.
2 red would affect St. Louis, through fear of a
squeeze, while Minneapolis and Chicago might take
no notice of it. Now that No. 2 hard winter is deliverable on contracts in Chicago, that market will
at times be the lowest, relatively, of all the markets;
and while there may be manipulation—heavy buying
and selling by some big interests—there is little dan-
ger of any more actual corners there in wheat.

With a crop such as the one raised in 1903 (the
government report on December 28th estimated it
at 637,000,000 bushels), the exports will be principally in the form of flour. The largely increased
consumption in this country makes what was a large
crop some years ago, a small one now. Therefore
the price of wheat will, until the production is in-

creased, be governed by the milling demand more than ever before. While, of course, the different markets must keep within certain relative limits— manipulation not interfering—past differences can- not be used as a guide. This seems particularly true of Western markets as compared with New York and Liverpool, for the latter two are based on wheat as a shipping product rather than wheat as a milling product. Owing to the fact that Liverpool prices are based on wheat for import, that ocean rates are continually fluctuating, while prices in several of the important markets in this country are largely in- fluenced by milling demand, and furthermore that flour is often being sold for export when wheat can- not—when these conditions are considered, Liver- pool does not seem to deserve an all-powerful influ- ence as a price-regulator.

THE DIFFERENT OPTIONS.

The same futures in the various markets also show a great difference owing to the winter wheat and the spring wheat crop movements beginning at dif- ferent times. The July futures in Chicago and St. Louis, being "new crop" options, that is, new wheat being delivered in that month, those markets are cheaper than Minneapolis July. The latter, owing to a great scarcity of No. 1 northern wheat, might rule very high, while, with a big winter wheat crop, Chicago July might sell extremely low.

September is a new crop month in Minneapolis, but in case of a late harvest and a delayed move- ment, due to rains, that market might be higher, rel- atively, than any other.

The December and May options are, with the exceptions noted, on an equal footing in all markets,—
that is, there are no crop or other natural differences.

THE CURB.

Chicago is the only market where trading on the
curb ("unofficial" trading after the close of the session, or from 1 :15 to 3 o'clock) and trading in privileges is not permitted. There is a state law in Illi-
nois prohibiting the trading in puts and calls, but
this will doubtless be repealed within the next few
years. After the Chicago Board of Trade frowned
upon curb and privilege trading, Milwaukee developed a wide market for this class of trading. At
the present time, however, trading in wheat is only
permitted for fifteen minutes after the close of the
session, though privileges are traded in until 3 :00
o'clock, and also at all times during the session. In
Minneapolis there is a curb for fifteen minutes before the opening every morning. After the session, until 3 :00 o'clock (2 :00 o'clock on Saturday)
both wheat and privileges are traded in, and at
times large amounts of grain are traded in then;
but practically nothing is done in the morning in
privileges.

The curb has not been dignified by the unanimous
approval of the trade, yet as actual commercial transactions and speculative deals are so interwoven in
the buying and selling of grain futures that one
could not exist without the other, it seems like hair-
splitting to draw the line at the curb.

However this may be, both the speculator and
the elevator owner often find privilege trading useful

and the curb a great convenience. As any one who is not familiar with the details of such transactions can readily become so through his broker, it would be superfluous to explain them here. It seems sufficient to generalize.

It sometimes happens that great strength or marked weakness on the curb does not indicate the tendency of the market the following day. As a rule, the trader will gain nothing in buying or selling on the curb, unless to close a transaction. But when the curb shows a good advance or decline from the closing price, it is generally a good plan to take profits on long or short wheat; for, unless it is during a wild market, the price will, the following day, probably sell back to near the closing price. Then, if the trader desires, he can replace his line at a profit. The trader should, in fact, harden his heart against becoming either bullish or bearish because of anything done on the curb. He should remember that the curb is a very narrow market, therefore one scared short or long can create a small-sized panic. This is more noticeable on Saturdays or before a holiday, for then "the crowd" has evened up, and no one cares to open new trades.

What is true of prices on the curb is true of privileges. One illustration will suffice to show this.

On December 12, 1903, there was heavy buying of calls all day in Milwaukee, and it was estimated that 1,500,000 were bought. No particular attention was given this during the day, and it had no effect, at first, on the Minneapolis curb. Minneapolis May wheat closed at $81\frac{1}{4}$c, and calls started at $81\frac{1}{2}$-$\frac{5}{8}$c, and were for a time traded in at that price. Soon after the close of the market, however, the representative of a Chicago house received an order to buy calls (1,000,000, it was thought). He bid the price up to 82¼, and finally succeeded in buying about three-quarters of a million. By this time there was general interest and some little excitement on the curb. Others began bidding for calls, and 82¾ was paid for one lot of 100.

The buying of calls on such a scale both in Milwaukee and Minneapolis naturally caused a great deal of surmising by the traders as to what it meant. It was thought that it might be a blind, to cause firmness the following morning so that some one might sell a large amount of wheat, or that a bull market was being anticipated. Yet the market the next day was uneventful, and it was then concluded that the Milwaukee traders who sold the calls, bought in Minneapolis as a hedge, to protect themselves.

Now this instance is mentioned to show that conservatism is always in order with the trader. He should never permit himself to become stampeded. Had any one bought wheat on the curb because of the activity and seeming strength, and doubtless some did, they would have found themselves in at the top of a bulge next day—the one thing every trader should be the most intent upon avoiding.

Some traders never buy nor sell privileges, while others are continually dealing in them. Some buy them, but seldom or never sell them. Others may sell oftener than purchase. A use to which they are put by some, is as a protection to their trades. For example, a trader has 10,000 bushels of wheat on which there is a profit. He therefore buys 10 puts, the same as one might buy insurance, and so limits his loss for the next day, yet has all the advantage of any advance there may be. One may also buy puts with the expectation of buying wheat the following day, using the puts as a stop-loss order. They are also bought, of course, when one expects a sharp decline. Calls are bought on just the reverse of these conditions. While, in the long run, the average trader may not make much money in buying privileges, it is safer than to sell them. The inexperienced trader should be exceedingly cautious about selling them, for, if the wheat is put to, or called of, him, he is likely to meet with a loss many times greater than the amount received for the privileges.

CHAPTER IX.

THE CHART AS AN AID IN TRADING.

The chart is a picture of the fluctuations of grain or stocks, and is valuable to any one who follows the market, whether broker, trader, cash grain man, banker or commercial editor. It shows at a glance, just as any other picture does, what one would otherwise be obliged to read or study tables to discover. Some men depend upon their memory for the picture of the market fluctuations, and carry the principal deviations "in their heads." But this can, of course, only be done while the conditions are fresh in mind, and one must necessarily forget many important features from month to month and from year to year. Charts of the different grain options and of stocks, when kept for a series of years, become invaluable to the trader as records.

Besides their value merely as a picture of passing events and as records, charts are used by many traders as a guide to their transactions. Other traders who do not use them follow the same principle, or theory, in trading; as, buying when the price has twice declined to the same point, or selling after it has advanced two or more times to a given point without passing, or "breaking through" it; buying on an advancing market after a break of half the advance, etc. If the price declines to 70c, say, reacts, again declines and reacts, traders are quick to con-

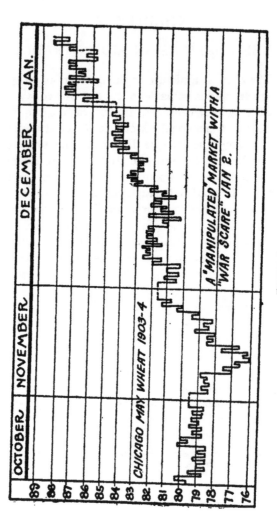

FIGURE A.

clude this a safe price at which to buy; and it does not require a chart to show this to men who are watching the market. Yet several weeks later, the incident may be forgotten by nine-tenths of those who noticed it. The chart, however, never permits one to forget, hence its usefulness.

In making a chart, it is necessary, in order to give its full value, to record all the principal fluctuations each day. The high and low points are not sufficient. In keeping a chart of the wheat market, the writer believes that all fluctuations of ⅜c should be kept, except during very active markets. If nothing smaller than ½c is used, valuable suggestions are sometimes lost. A separate chart showing only the 1c and greater fluctuations is kept by some, and this is worth the extra work. In charts of stocks, nothing smaller than one point is recorded.

THE CHART THEORY.

Some traders have devised a theory on trading by the chart, and it must be confessed that there are many good ideas embodied in it, yet no one should be deceived for a moment in thinking that there is any "highway to success" in speculation, other than by the same amount of good common sense and long experience required to succeed in other lines of business.

No trader can follow, inflexibly, the theory of chart trading without occasionally getting "whip-sawed" in a way he will think is wicked.

To briefly explain the chart theory, reference will be made to Figure A, which is a chart of Chicago May wheat from October 19, 1903, when trading began to be general in that option, to January 6, 1904, just after the first Russian-Japanese "war-scare" had had its effect on the market by scaring in the shorts.

Up to the last of October the December was the active option and the fluctuations in the May were, for the six weeks, narrow. As 78 to 80c seemed high for May wheat in the fall, there was heavy short selling and a great amount of hedging in this option. Yet the chart shows that at 78½c there was steady buying. Hence this is the story the chart tells to the experienced eye: Some one was accumulating a big line of wheat at 78½ to 79½c. At this time it was not known that a certain big Chicago speculator was engineering what was to be one of the most successful bull scalping campaigns the world has ever seen, yet the chart plainly shows that some one was supporting the market at 78½c. Later, it was estimated that this big long carried a line of 20,000,000 to 25,000,000 bushels.

Now, in theory, wheat was a purchase at around 78½c, for a scalp of ½ to ¾c. Also wheat would be a purchase should it go above 80c, for then it would be in new ground and show that the buying strength was greater than the selling. On the other hand, it would be a sale (short) should it break below 78c, for that would demonstrate that the bears had prevailed. The first indication of which way it might go was in the first part of November, when it sold down to 78¼c and failed, after three up-turns, to again reach 79c. This was a warning to the longs to get out of the market, and a notice to the bears to take a chance on the short side.

When the break came and the price passed through 78c, the tardy longs had the choice of either taking a small loss or holding their wheat with the chance of a big one. It was almost a certainty that there would be a further decline. The decline that followed was thought to be a shake-out, yet the chart showed nothing to encourage the buyer until the price was checked at 76c. All news was then bearish, as it usually is during a slump. The price reacted ½c and again declined almost to 76c. Now when it started up from 76⅛c after failing to reach 76c, it was a notice that the decline had, at least temporarily, been checked. Almost perfect double "bottoms" were formed—a strong point. The quick and decisive trader would have bought wheat at 76½ to 76¾c or possibly at 76¼c, with the intention of selling and taking his loss if it broke below 76c. Yet if the chart trader had failed to buy on the second turn-up, he would have watched intently for the next opportunity. This came on the decline from 77⅝c to 76¾c. This decline terminated before reaching the last "top," which is at 76½c.

The advance that followed terminated at 78⅝c, and as that had, the first part of the month, been a selling point, in fact, almost where the late slump started from,—the trader would naturally take profits here, and await further developments. The reaction stopped at 78c, and double bottoms were formed there, which was a notice that the long who was causing the advance came to the support of the market here. This would give courage to the small traders, and though they might take profits at 79c, the advance the latter part of November, after passing through 80c, was sufficient notice that the big bull was in control to induce buying by the chart trader.

The next decline came at 81⅝c, the first of December. This was only a "natural reaction," which every conservative trader was expecting after an advance of 5½c without a reaction of a cent. The chart gave no warning of its approach, yet, except during run-away markets, which seldom come, there is hardly ever, one might say never, a steady advance greater than this without a reaction of at least a cent. The big long sold wheat freely at this point, and the trade gossip of this date, now a part of market history, consists largely of his doings. The chart shows that he bought in his line again at 80¼ to 80½c.

At this point the three bottoms are somewhat irregular, and might confuse the trader but for one thing, namely, that the price was now in new ground, and that the old high point, in October, was just above 80c. This is shown more clearly on a chart which gives no fluctuations of less than 1c. Therefore, according to the chart theory, 80 to 80½c was a safe place to buy; for, if it was really an advancing market, the decline would be stopped at the old tops. The chart shows that it was, and the next advance carried it up to 82¾c. The numerous tops at 82⅝ to 82¾c clearly indicate that wheat was sold in sufficient amounts to cause a reaction. This was warning enough to the chart trader to take profits and to buy only on the breaks, or to keep out in an-

ticipation of a big break. However, should the price
advance through 83c instead of breaking sharply—
no one could tell which it might do—it would then
be a purchase. Yet as there had been an advance
of 6¾c and as 82¼c is regarded as a good price,
the conservative trader would rather expect the
break which came the middle of December. The
decline was again checked at 80¼c, thus forming
a double bottom with the previous break. Another
bottom was formed at 80¾c and another at 80⅝c,
which should have encouraged the bulls to buy. An
advance of 3c followed, then came more profit-tak-
ing, at 83½c, by the big long, and buying back his
line at 82¾c, and another advance and a new high
point at 84⅞c.

There was now a great deal of "war talk," as this
was when Russia and Japan were making active pre-
parations for trouble. Yet it was known all the time
that there was a big short interest in the market
(some Wall Street traders who had been induced to
get into a wheat deal). Should the market continue
to advance, they must soon start to cover, and this
would cause a run-away market. At around 84½c
the big long sold wheat, but bought it back at 84c,
thus scalping out some good profits.

By the last of December, the war outlook was om-
inous. January 1st came on Friday, a holiday, of
course, and Saturday was a short day, and with Sunday following, the shorts were in a fever. They
started to run on Saturday morning, January 2nd,
and the chart shows the result. Although wheat was
theoretically a purchase if it passed 85c, there was

no opportunity to purchase it until it got above 86c, the advance was so rapid.

The big shorts bought in several million bushels of wheat at the advance, and the big long took profits at around 87½c, but on Monday, the 4th, he again bought, and the chart shows where he supported the market, at 86½c. Yet, according to the chart, wheat was a sale at 87½c, though as the market had been supported at 86½c, the trader would expect support again at that point, or, if not there, certainly at the other bottoms at 85¾c. On January 5th the market broke to 85¾c and was supported there by good buying. This should have encouraged buying, yet had it broken below that point, it would indicate still lower prices.

In a general way, the foregoing gives an idea of the chart theory. By following it, one will likely avoid buying on the bulges, and will be encouraged to buy on the weak places.

SYSTEMATIC TRADING.

Unquestionably, the average trader loses many opportunities and a large percentage of the profits actually to his credit at one time or another, by not working systematically. The writer hesitates about using the word "systematically," lest some one may confuse it with trading by "system." There is a wide difference. One may, and should, trade "systematically," yet not attempt to follow any "system." The writer has never investigated any of the so-called systems, designed to beat the market, for the reason that he has never heard of any successful and prosperous trader who works on that principle. Nor does he believe that human weaknesses can be overcome by the aid of mathematical rules.

In another chapter, mention is made of scalping with half the trader's line, whether grain or stocks, either on an advancing or a declining market. This gives a suggestion of what is meant by systematic trading. It is not regarded as expert trading, for instance, where one buys, say 10 wheat at 70c and sells it at 80c. It would be a good investment, to be sure, and show conservative judgment. Yet the expert who has sufficient confidence in his own judgment to hold for a 10c profit, would have increased his line after having say 3c profit, followed it up with a stop order, and possibly increased his line again at about 5c profit. Also, some would have doubled the line after having 2c profit, and then have scalped with 10 wheat, or half the line, selling that much on every bulge, and buying it back on any break. Often, on a slowly advancing market, scalps of ½ to 1c can thus be made. Sometimes, of course, a spurt of a cent or two will come when the trader has but half his line, but there will always be reactions enough to get in again.

This is systematic trading, yet it is not following a system. It is merely using good trading sense. This plan may also be profitably followed when one expects an advance, or decline, though the market drags for several weeks, fluctuating within narrow limits. On such a market, should one buy, or sell, and then wait for the expected advance or decline to come, he might become tired and disgusted, and finally close out just at the wrong time.

This is especially likely to happen in the fall or winter when, under normal conditions, prices of grain are steady, with a lower tendency, though with numerous ½c fluctuations. At such a time, any but the most persistent investment buyer will get discouraged by long waiting, not only for the expected advance but for the lowest price; for every one wants to buy on the bottom. This sometimes happens, but by chance only. Under such conditions, the following plan is a good one to follow: it was suggested by an expert trader with especial reference to the corn market, but of course the same principle can be applied to anything else as well, when it is believed the price has almost touched bottom:

SCALPING FOR HALF CENT PROFITS.

"Buy a small portion of your usual line, say 5,000 bushels, at 42⅝. If the market declines, buy 5,000 more at 42⅛, and again at 41⅝. If the market recovers from 41⅝ (or from 41⅜ or 41½, or wherever it may sell to after you buy at 41⅝) to 42⅛, sell what you bought at 41⅝, taking ½c profit. If market sells to 42⅝, sell what you bought at 42⅛, replacing each lot sold as the market again declines, buying on ½c declines. Take profits of ½c whenever offered. Never take less, nor strive for more. Sometimes you will get more. For instance, you have corn bought at 41⅝ and have in an order to sell at 42⅛. Market closes at 42@42⅛ and your selling order can not be executed. Next day the market opens at 42¼—you get ⅝c profit. Replace your corn at 41⅝ (not 41¾); market may close at 41⅝c-¾c and your order to buy at 41⅝ not be filled that day. Next day market may open at 41½ and your buying order be filled at that price. Sell out this purchase at 42⅛, not 42.

"If after first purchase at 42⅝, market advances to 43⅛, credit yourself with ½c profit, but do not sell out your corn. Mark the cost of it up to 43⅛ and buy a like amount again at 42⅝. Always keep on hand the original purchase, but mark it up as each ½c advance is recorded.

"If market declines to 39⅛ or under, it will not do so without numerous reactions of ½c, and the many profits secured will greatly reduce the loss in the accumulated purchases. In fact, they might amount to more than this loss. In the advent of any sensational or positive bull news at any time during the accumulation of this corn, all orders to sell on the half-cent advances could be cancelled and the whole line carried up. If after the first purchase the market should advance to a point from which you might consider it not safe to accumulate on each half-cent decline, you could sell out and wait for a price that would suit. You will see that if you trade in this manner, one standing open order is all you need to enter."

In the foregoing case, it was thought the price at 42⅝ was about low point, that there was little possibility of its going to 39⅛.

QUICK DECISION NECESSARY.

Above all else, the trader should study trading, so that no matter what circumstances arise, he will not become demoralized—get "rattled." At any moment, he should be in a position, and a mental condition, to decide without hesitation to close his trades at a loss, take profits, sell half his line or add to it.

To illustrate this point, an incident that came to the writer's attention on Jan. 2, 1904, is given. A trader, on the bull side, had carried but 10 wheat over the holiday, Jan. 1., as he had become discouraged at the refusal of the price (see chart of "A manipulated market with a war-scare," on another page) to advance above 84¾c. But he reasoned that should it go through 85c, there was but one thing to do—buy more wheat. A few minutes after the opening, Chicago May touched 85c, and the trader unhesitatingly gave his order to buy 30,000. The advance was so rapid, due to the war-scare, that his order was executed at 86½c. Then the market steadied, and after the first rush of buying, settled back to 85¾c. The trader reasoned that this was a normal reaction after such an advance, and so bought 10 more, at 85⅞c. In a few minutes the second advance began, which the trader reasoned must come if it was really a bull market, and carried the price to 87¾c. Here it hesitated, sagged down to 87c and slowly advanced again, but not with the early vim.

Now what should a trader do under such circumstances. He could clear a profit of between $700 and $800, made in an hour's time, or hold his trades until Monday. With further war news, another sharp advance would follow, but without it, the market might sell off sharply. This was self-evident, but the trader reasoned further; he took into account the mental strain incident to the uncertainty, and so concluded that a good profit safely secured, and peace of mind over Sunday, were worth more than the chance of a bigger profit on Monday. He therefore closed his trades—and on Monday the market sold off 1½c.

CONCLUSION.

In writing on speculation, one can go only about so far without traveling in a circle. While the circle might be made greater or less, eventually it must be completed where it began; and that is with the prevailing tendency of human nature to speculate. The writer has chosen as a motto the words that appear on the cover, "There is no gain without some risk." This should be kept in mind by every prospective trader. As it is human nature to want money, so it is to speculate; and it is folly to preach against it. Investment and speculation are the only ways open to the salaried man and the wage earner ever to get ahead in the game of life. Every man owes it to himself and to his family to become as prosperous as his capacity will allow. If his business sense tells him that the savings bank, the farm mortgage and the bond are the surest roads to prosperity, they are the routes for him to travel. If greater opportunities are desired, the speculative field will naturally be turned to; but the man should make as close a study of it as of his everyday occupation.

POSTSCRIPT.

ARMOUR'S TWO MAY WHEAT CAMPAIGNS.

(Written for the Commercial West on Jan. 27, 1904.)

When one studies the trails made by the "great manipulator," Armour, in his May wheat deals, as Ernest Thompson Seton would study the trail of a jack-rabbit in the snow, a startling similarity is noticed between that of a year ago and the present one. The accompanying chart shows, on the right, the culmination of the 1902-3 manipulation. The one to the left shows the present deal.

Just when last year's deal was started, it is impossible to say, but some one began to accumulate a line of May wheat in August, 1902, at 69 to 70c, following it up in September, at around 70c, and the first half of October, at 70 to 71c. It is probable that Armour acquired his line during this period, when every one else was selling.

The first real advance started on Oct. 13, 1903, and then followed a four-months' scalping campaign on a magnificent scale, but far inferior to the one that has now been in progress since Nov. 1, 1904. During the campaign of a year ago there were three big shake-outs and two smaller ones, besides the usual minor fluctuations. But the market did not show the systematic scalping on a large scale that has been such a marked feature of the present campaign. In fact, last year's deal compares with the present one as an amateurish job compares with a professional one. One of the weaknesses last year was in permitting Chicago to get out of line with other markets early in the game. When the climax came, Chicago

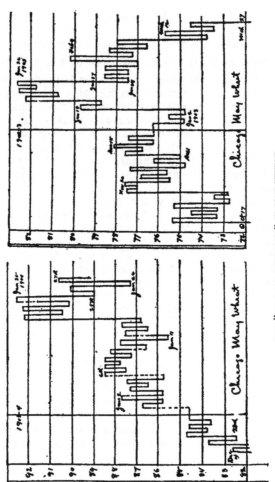

THE "ARMOUR PARALLEL" IN MAY WHEAT.

was 3¾c over Minneapolis, and had been 1½ to 2c over all the time. This year, Minneapolis, early in the campaign, was made to lead Chicago, selling as high as 1¾c over. St. Louis was strong all the time, and Duluth and Kansas City had the needed stimulants ejected into them to keep them well in line. In fact, Chicago was relatively the weakest of the western markets through the early winter. It was comparatively easy to keep the smaller markets strong, and these in turn made it easy to control Chicago.

While the general plan of both deals, as shown by the course of prices, is similar, and the January climax of each almost identical, there were more sharp advances in the first campaign, and heavier slugging on the bulges, showing less deftness in handling the deal. In the first, the bears were hammered to death with a club; in the second they were strangled, with politeness and consideration. In a 9c advance, in the second campaign, from Nov. 12 to Dec. 30, there was but one shake-out of 2c.

As a scalping campaign, it is hardly possible that the one of 1903-4 has ever been equaled. Armour's line of wheat was variously estimated at from 15,000,000 to 25,000,000 bushels; and it was, apparently, accumulated in October, at 78 to 79c, when all the world was selling May wheat. When it broke to 76c, Nov. 1 to 12, the bears were emboldened to sell more, and 70c was then the talk. On the advance which followed, to Dec. 30, there were 32 points at which it seemed certain that Armour was a seller, and as many where he bought back his wheat at a lower price. The greatest break was 2c, and there were but six others of 1c or more. The last of December, it was estimated that the big trader's line was as great as at any time. Then, on Jan. 2, came the war-scare, which put wheat from 84⅝c to 87¾c

in one day. The accompanying chart shows the
price fluctuations since then to the 27th.

The particularly interesting feature, when
comparing the two campaigns, is the striking
similarity as shown in the accompanying charts
—and the uncertainty of the outcome of the present one. A year ago, it was asserted that on Jan.
27 and 28, Armour sold 15,000,000 to 20,000,000
bushels of wheat. It was simply dumped into the
pit by a score of brokers. Then, there was a
large outside trade; and the price was 10c lower
than now; yet it broke only 5c.

This year, the top price was 92c instead of 82c,
when the break came; there was very little outside trade, and the scalpers were bearish. Therefore, when Armour began selling, every one else
in the pit followed, and there were no buyers.
The result was that the big trader could not un-
load (if that was his desire), and, in fact, is
thought to have sold but 3,000,000 to 4,000,000
bushels; yet the price broke 5c. On the second
day's slump, he turned buyer; some believe he
found it necessary, in order to keep the market
from smashing all to pieces. The quick recovery
of 3c on the 26th was due to his support.

The basis for the present campaign is the
shortage of contract wheat throughout the country, and not an actual shortage of wheat.

FOREIGN MARKET FLUCTUATIONS.

By referring to the table which follows, the foreign market fluctuations on grain can readily be changed to apply to our own weights and money. For instance, should the cables report from Paris, "Wheat 10 centimes lower," a glance at the table shows that Paris quotes on 100 kilos, or 3.67 bushels, and that 10 centimes decline on that amount is equal to ½c on one bushel.

Berlin quotations are on 1,000 kilos, equal to 36.74 bushels; and the money quotations are pfennigs and marks.

The exchange hours of the foreign markets are: Liverpool, from 1 to 3 p. m., which, in Minneapolis time, is 8:30 to 10:30 a. m.; Berlin, 1 to 3 p. m., or, in Minneapolis, 6 to 8 a. m.; Paris, 2 to 4 p. m., or, in Minneapolis, 8 to 10 a. m.

LIVERPOOL Quotes values per 100 lbs. or cental		BERLIN Quotes per 100 Kilos equal to 36.74 bushelse		ANTWERP, PARIS Quote on 100 Kilos qual to 3.67 bushels	
100 lbs or cental Penny	60 lbs. or bushel Cent	1000 Kilos Pfennings	One Bushel Cent.	100 Kilos Centimes	One Bushel Cent.
¼d	¼@⅜c	12½ pf	⅛c	5 cen	¼c
½d	⅝@¾c	25 pf	⅛@¼c	10 cen	½c
¾d	⅞c	37½ pf	¼c	15 cen	¾c
1 d	1⅛@¼c	50 pf	¼@⅜c	20 cen	1 c
1¼d	1½c	75 pf	½c	25 cen	1¼@⅜c
1½d	1¾@⅞c	1 mk	⅝c	30 cen	1½c
1¾d	2⅛c	1¼ mk	¾@⅞c	35 cen	1¾c
2 d	2⅜@½c	1½ mk	1c	40 cen	2c
2¼d	2⅝@¾c	2 mk	1¼c	50 cen	2⅝c
2½d	3c	2½ mk	1⅝c	60 cen	3⅛c
2¾d	3¼@⅜c	3 mk	1⅞@2c	70 cen	3⅞@4c
3 d	3⅝c	3½ mk	2¼c	80 cen	4⅛@¼c

CPSIA information can be obtained
at www.ICGtesting.com
Printed in the USA
BVHW06s2016120618
518859BV00012B/98/P